BEFORE AND AFTER

or

THE RELATIONS OF THE RACES AT THE SOUTH

BEFORE AND AFTER

❖ *OR* ❖

THE RELATIONS OF THE RACES

AT THE SOUTH

BY
Isaac DuBose Seabrook

edited with an introduction by

John Hammond Moore

BATON ROUGE
LOUISIANA STATE UNIVERSITY PRESS

EDITOR'S ACKNOWLEDGMENTS

I would like to thank E. L. Inabinett, director of the South Caroliniana Library, for permission to print this essay. Mrs. Luther B. Lockhart of Atlanta kindly loaned me a photograph of her uncle, Isaac DuBose Seabrook, and discussed at length her recollections of him. Others who helped piece together this story include Kennard R. Bowers, Samuel G. Stoney, and Mrs. Granville Prior, all of Charleston; Mrs. Leila H. Price of Wadmalaw Island; E. Percival Seabrook and Mrs. Clara Mae Jacobs, both of Columbia; W. Porter Ware of Sewanee, Tennessee; and Mrs. Germaine Reed of Atlanta.

JOHN HAMMOND MOORE

CONTENTS

BEFORE AND AFTER

or

THE RELATIONS OF THE RACES AT THE SOUTH

INTRODUCTION

Isaac DuBose Seabrook
and the Emergence of Jim Crow in South Carolina

In 1895 Isaac DuBose Seabrook, an aristocratic Charleston, South Carolina, bachelor then working as a hotel clerk, wrote a book-length essay on the subject of race relations in the South. The essay never found its way into print in Seabrook's lifetime. But it survived him, and is here published for the first time.

It is almost impossible to read what Seabrook has to say about race relations without comparing his words with those of other men of his troubled era. The obscure Charlestonian had pored over the liberal writings of George Washington Cable, but rejected the famous teller of Creole tales as an impractical dreamer. Judge Albion W. Tourgée of Reconstruction fame he found confusing and contradictory. Although Seabrook apparently had not read Lewis H. Blair's *Prosperity of the South Dependent Upon the Elevation of the Negro* (1889), it is obvious that both of these aristocrats—one from Charleston and the other from Richmond—would have had much to talk about had they ever met. Yet, any encounter might well have proved disappointing. Seabrook was far less affluent, less optimistic concerning trends in race relations, but perhaps more realistic. He had played and worked with Negroes. He knew, perhaps as well as any white man of his time could, their needs and capabilities; at least he seems to have known the

3

individual Negro far better than Blair, who viewed the world from the polished windows of his East Grace Street mansion.

That Richmond merchant, according to C. Vann Woodward's fine edition of Blair's plea for Negro rights, was an iconoclast who with gusto and delight "pitched into his attack on cherished and hallowed Southern myths, prejudice, credos, anything that stood in the way of the new social doctrine he preached." [1] It is not too surprising to discover that, having expressed thoughts which even today make thousands of Virginians shudder, Blair recoiled from his own words before he died in 1916. Seabrook, on the other hand, was not doing battle with his native South, merely trying with cold, reasoned logic to make it see the error of its ways. Perhaps before he died he too regretted some of his statements; but, since his essay was never published, he did not have to recant. Part of his thesis concerning race relations would appeal to any stalwart mid-twentieth-century conservative who says "Go slow" when he means "Do nothing . . . go nowhere." Yet only part of Seabrook's essay would find approval among the Bull Connors, Jim Clarks, and Ross Barnetts who still inhabit high places. For, while bewailing the passing of a master class (which presumably understood the Negro) and of a Negro who knew "his place," Seabrook was a firm advocate of federal aid to education and came to conclusions which undoubtedly would have troubled many Americans in the 1890's, as well as some in the 1960's.

Unlike most spokesmen of his day and many leaders of our own age, he did not view education as a magic potion capable of curing all ills. Education might (or might not) alleviate prejudice, but it could not eradicate it. Racial antipathy, he wrote, is based upon many factors. "All these factors may be called prejudice, pride, obstinancy, vanity. They may be so; but, in any case, it is to be remembered that prejudices are very real things, very potent powers in the life of each person and probably still more potent in the life of a society, and so grow by mutual sympathy. It is clear that the education of either race does not directly touch on any of these things."

[1] Woodward (ed.), *A Southern Prophecy: The Prosperity of the South Dependent Upon the Elevation of the Negro* by Lewis H. Blair (Boston, 1964), xxvii.

Education, in Seabrook's words, "is not a specific against prejudice and evil passions." And the work to be done in the South was so vast! As he wrote in 1895, about 15 per cent of the white population and 60 per cent of the colored over ten years of age were illiterate.

Great forests and tracts of humanity, as it were, are not claimed for civilization. These great masses of ignorance are part of the citizens of these states and may at any time become (and are at times) a source of danger to society. As a matter [of] self-defence, if for no other causes, these masses ought to [be] educated. And now arises the difficulty and in an unlooked for quarter. Will they receive it? A man to be educated must toil in getting it. Study is not purely receptive. Minds are not empty jugs into which knowledge can be poured until they are full. The process of learning is equally [as] arduous as the work of the hoe and the plough, to many persons far more so and to even the most intelligent is far from being the amusement of a summer day. Into the grove of learning the most of us have been ushered, with not a few tears, by means of rods cut from its boughs.
A man must desire learning before he can receive it. He must understand its uses; he must see the need of it in the affairs of life. Unfortunately this is not true of the Negroes of the South. With the mass of them the simplicity of life is too great; their occupations are too few and too simple; their circle of activity is too narrow; their connection with the life of the cities is too infrequent and too incomplete to awake in their minds any due sense of the value of reading and writing even— to say nothing of the most extended education. The desire of education among them must go hand in hand with the improvements of their material condition, with better homes, with more diversified and skilled work, with better morals, and increased self-interest. There is no short method by which it can be made to precede these things, any more than rain can be produced from a dry atmosphere without the presence of clouds.

Seabrook, like Lewis Blair, felt that the Negro of the South should be elevated, but he conceded this might be a long, hard struggle— perhaps it would take a century or more. In his concluding pages Seabrook listed three prerequisites for continued improvement among Negroes: 1) They must remain in day-to-day contact with the white race. Separation would, as he saw it, end the beneficial influence of the white man. 2) The limits of Negro improvement must be the same as those of the whites, or at least there should be no barriers to prevent elevation from continuing indefinitely. 3) The numerical increase of Negroes in any section of the nation must not be so great as to create "black" states.

But it is perhaps unfair to compare the writings of Lewis Blair and Isaac Seabrook. Not only did Blair view the world from a different level, but Virginia was hardly South Carolina. In the late nineteenth century South Carolina's Negroes were less educated and proportionally more numerous than those of the Old Dominion. Even the dates when these two men wrote have relevance. Blair composed his work in 1888; Seabrook, his in 1895. Blair could see menacing clouds on the horizon. Jim Crow laws were, for the most part, merely a threat. By the time Seabrook put together his essay the full fury of the storm was apparent to everyone, especially to citizens of South Carolina living under the agrarian despotism of Benjamin Ryan Tillman. In fact, it was obviously the temper of the times which prompted Seabrook to write down his personal views concerning race relations.

Isaac DuBose Seabrook was born in Charleston on February 4, 1855, the son of Marian DuBose and Ephraim Mikell Seabrook. His father, member of a distinguished Edisto Island family and a graduate of South Carolina College, served several terms in the state legislature in the late 1840's, was private secretary to his uncle, Governor Whitemarsh Seabrook (1848–50), and was elected to the Secession Convention of 1860 from St. Luke's Parish, Beaufort District, where he had substantial plantations.[2] He served as a colonel in the Civil War and, after trying unsuccessfully to raise crops in 1867 and 1868, became clerk of the United States District Court in Charleston, a position he held for more than twenty years. Colonel Seabrook died while visiting in Atlanta in 1895, the year that Isaac wrote this essay.[3]

[2] According to the 1860 census, Seabrook, a thirty-seven-year-old planter, had real estate valued at $44,000 and personal property valued at $36,000. His wife, four young children (including Isaac, age five), and his mother lived with him in St. Luke's Parish, Beaufort.
[3] See the Charleston *News and Courier*, November 25, 1895, for his obituary.

The colonel was married three times, but had surviving children only by his second wife. In addition to Isaac, there were Julius, Katherine, and Marian. Since both Isaac and his brother graduated from college and one sister (Marian, or "Marie" as she was called) attended the Boston Conservatory of Music, one can conclude the family fared rather well during Reconstruction.

A devout Episcopalian—he wrote a history of the Protestant Episcopal Church of Edisto Island and was frequently a delegate to religious conferences—Colonel Seabrook sent both boys to the University of the South.[4] During a half dozen years on that high Tennessee plateau young Isaac got a thorough indoctrination in the classics, studying Gibbon, Tacitus, and Locke. He served as orator and as president of the Pi Omega Literary Society, and after receiving an A.B. degree (1875) taught for two years in the university's grammar school. In the summer of 1877 he returned to Charleston, where for the next half century he seems to have lived a rather uneventful but financially precarious existence. Always a student of history and an avid collector of published material relating to his native state, he was by turns a phosphate miner, hotel clerk, part-time employee of the district court, "canvasser" of some sort, salesman, and dealer in prints and rare books.

According to various relatives who remember him, Isaac—or "DuBose" as he was more frequently known—was a favorite of a grandmother who granted nearly all of his wishes, even going to Sewanee to be near him while he was a student and teacher. He was considered handsome, and, as a niece remarked, "had wit and ego enough to make an interesting personality." DuBose apparently had little sympathy with the women's rights movement; he "felt that the male stalked the earth as a god and especially felt superiority over the female." One cousin noted that he was either "too smart to work" or thought himself "too much of a gentleman to accept confining employment." Another, viewing Seabrook with more sympathy, observed that "he probably belonged in a college atmosphere instead of the business world," adding that he frequently turned to his brother Julius (an employee of the district court for many years) "when the going got rough."

4 Also, appointment in the summer of 1871 of William Porcher DuBose (1836–1918), a relative of his mother, as the university's chaplain may have influenced Isaac to go to Sewanee.

These observations, his rather erratic career, and an inventory of his estate when he died in 1928, shed some light on what sort of man Isaac DuBose Seabrook was. Julius noted as administrator that his elder brother left $164.45 in a local bank account, "a lot of books," and some personal effects. These items were subsequently sold for about $250. Among them were some one hundred books which Gittman's Book Store in Columbia bought for $45 on January 20, 1929. Although Gittman's no longer has records of this transaction, it is quite possible that among these volumes was the handwritten manuscript of "Before and After; or, The Relations of the Races at the South," which the South Caroliniana Library obtained from a California book dealer in 1946.

Seabrook's only published literary efforts seem to have been poems which occasionally appeared in the Charleston *News and Courier*. One of these, "The Dome of St. Michael's," was written to commemorate the Easter season of 1922. However, throughout the first two decades of this century, despite whatever line of work he was engaged in, this enigmatic man was always interested in books and prints. Papers of Yates Snowden and A. S. Salley, Jr., at the South Caroliniana Library reveal that Seabrook occasionally sold items to both of these prominent historians. He seems to have been on especially good terms with Snowden. His letters to that gentleman frequently open with Greek quotations, and one undated note contains this tantalizing comment:

Many thanks for the Seabrook item. The stock seems to be improving. No telling what the African, transported to a better clime, may achieve in the future with the friendly help of a little . . . .

I. D. Seabrook.

This evidently refers to the general exodus of Negroes to the North during the opening years of the century, but the full meaning is not clear. Seabrook apparently was most active as a book dealer from 1900 to 1910. Working out of his home at 41 Queen Street, he frequently published lists of items for sale; and, if the Salley and Snowden papers are any indication, he also kept up a lively correspondence. In the early 1920's he and his brother Julius, also a bachelor, moved to 62 Logan Street. Seabrook is cited in the Charleston *City Directory* (1922) as a "book agent," but by 1926 he had retired. He died two years later, on December 21, 1928, following several months of declining health.[5]

This, then, is the man who wrote the essay which follows—or, at least, this is as much as we will probably ever know about him. Well-educated, refined in his tastes, Isaac DuBose Seabrook was never able to adjust to Henry Grady's New South. At no time was this inability to conform more apparent than when, as a clerk in the Mills House (perhaps merely to pass long hours while on desk duty), he composed this analysis of race relations.

It is no accident that Seabrook wrote in 1895. During the fall of that year South Carolina's political leaders, with a half dozen Negroes in their midst, sat under the watchful eye of "Pitchfork Ben" Tillman and put together the stern, white-supremist constitution which still governs the state today. The deliberations of that body, especially debates over the right of suffrage, filled scores of newspaper columns. What was being said and done in Columbia was a prime topic of conversation on the streets, in restaurants, bars, and hotel lobbies throughout the Palmetto State.

However, the constitutional convention which paved the way for Jim Crow and all that followed in his wake is merely the climax to, or perhaps more properly a major turning point in, a much longer story.[6] This tale has its genesis in Reconstruction and the constitution which carpetbaggers, scalawags, and Negroes bequeathed to South Carolina in 1868. Article x, section 10 of that document declared that public schools and state-supported colleges would be open to all regardless of color or race. Yet, because integration was utterly impractical so soon after the demise of slavery, by tacit agreement the state superintendent of public

[5] His obituary can be found in the Charleston *Evening Post*, December 22, 1928.

[6] For an excellent analysis of this era, see George Brown Tindall, *South Carolina Negroes, 1877–1900* (Columbia, 1952), especially pp. 291–302. This volume now in paperback (Baton Rouge, 1966). Joel Williamson, *After Slavery: The Negro in South Carolina During Reconstruction, 1861–1877* (Chapel Hill, 1965) details the prelude to those years. Together these two works give a thorough, although sometimes conflicting picture of the South Carolina Negro, 1861–1900. Williamson, benefiting from recent research and his own exhaustive scholarship, tends to see segregation as a reality *in fact* long before it becomes so *in law*.

education was permitted to establish and to operate a segregated system. When Negroes entered the University of South Carolina in 1873 nearly all of the white students packed up and left; and if colored youngsters had appeared at the doors of white public schoolhouses throughout the state, the whole system, begun only in 1870, undoubtedly would have collapsed.

Throughout the early 1870's the majority in the state legislature constantly reinforced civil rights laws in a vain attempt to shore up defenses as fast as they were breached by disgruntled South Carolinians. In 1870, Article I, section 39 of the constitution, prohibiting discrimination because of race and color, was strengthened by stating that "whatever authority has heretofore been conferred by law upon any free white person or persons to institute a suit" was now applicable to Negroes. In that same year segregation in theaters, places of amusement, and on "common carriers under public charter" was prohibited. Those convicted might be fined $1,000 or sentenced to serve up to six months in jail. Any corporation or licensed company practicing segregation was threatened with the loss of its franchise or license. If complaint came from "a colored or black person," burden of proof of innocence lay with the defendant. Five years later still another act provided that any business requiring a charter or license—whether or not it had such papers—could be held accountable for discriminatory practices. Obviously some individuals attempted to evade the letter of the law by failing to obtain permission to operate their businesses.[7]

Then, with Wade Hampton's Red Shirt campaign of 1876 and the return to power of white conservatives, the tide turned. Not too surprisingly, the first race bill (introduced in the state legislature in 1878) related to intermarriage; but it is somewhat of a surprise to discover there was substantial opposition from both colored and white legislators. While Negro spokesmen objected because the measure would dictate social usage, some whites thought it unconstitutional.[8] This bill was introduced in the senate, passed

[7] According to Tindall, *South Carolina Negroes*, 292–93, there were numerous complaints, but no convictions as a result of these statutes.
[8] During debate, according to the Columbia *Register*, December 10, 1878, one Negro representative drew laughter with these words: "I believe when God made us he intended for us to act and do as we pleased."

that body, but got bogged down in the lower chamber. Since test cases were before Virginia courts, legislators decided by a vote of 61 to 43 to carry the matter over to the next session.

Again, in December, 1879, house members urged delay. Some thought the measure unwise and unnecessary. One of its proponents pointed out that such restrictive laws in neighboring states caused a flow of "low and worthless" folk into South Carolina:

I don't know how it is in the other counties, and I will not undertake to say how many such are in York County; but I know that in Fort Mill township, wherein I reside, there are at least twenty-five or thirty white women living with colored men as husbands, and every one of them have come from North Carolina, and the colored man is the sufferer in every instance.

About two months ago a Negro man abducted a white girl only 12 years old from her parents in Mecklenberg County, N. C., brought her over in[to] South Carolina and married her. Her parents, finding out where they were in this State, sent an officer and had them arrested and the man put in the Charlotte jail.

Now, Mr. Speaker, if North Carolina has a right to do such things, surely South Carolina has a right to enact such laws as will protect her own society, and the people of the State, both white and black, demand this protection. I hope the bill will pass.[9]

And, pass it did, 87-22.

A year later Democrats began a revision of election laws which would culminate in the 1895 constitutional convention. Throughout May and June of 1882 voters had to register anew. If anyone failed to register or forgot to inform officials of a subsequent change of residence, even within a precinct, he could not vote. Of course, these provisions ensnared many Negro tenants and sharecroppers. In the election of 1882 voters faced eight different boxes for local, state, and congressional races. This was, in effect, a literacy test since the voter had to be able to read the label on each box; but it was not impossible for illiterate whites to get assistance, nor was it certain the order of boxes would not be changed from time to time to confuse Negroes informed as to sequence. Measures such as these were so successful that the

[9]Columbia *Register*, December 4, 1879.

Republican vote total of 91,780 in 1876 had dwindled to 13,740 by 1888.[10]

In 1883 the United States Supreme Court declared certain provisions of the Federal Civil Rights Act of 1875 unconstitutional. Negroes throughout the nation were alarmed for they interpreted this ruling (and they were right) as a green light to those who would wipe out state civil rights legislation. Two years later, while making an extensive commentary on Henry Grady's answer to an article published in *Century Magazine* by George Washington Cable, the Charleston *News and Courier* said the youthful Atlanta spokesman was correct when he wrote that the South would not accept Cable's views on "social intermingling." Nevertheless, Francis W. Dawson, editor of the Charleston daily, agreed that throughout the former Confederacy there was "a disposition everywhere to treat colored people with liberality and justice. It is accepted as an unchangeable fact that the political rights of the colored people will not and cannot be diminished, and also that miscegenation would be the ruin of the whites and blacks alike. Mr. Grady's main fault, we think, is in taking too cheerful a view of the situation as regards the assortment of the races. It will be harder, we fear, to prevent miscegenation than Mr. Grady thinks." [11]

Dawson, an Englishman who had come to America to fight for the South in the Civil War, emphasized that South Carolina's strong civil rights laws gave full protection to the Negro ballot. Colored citizens could get equal accommodations on trains in that state for equal price, but they usually chose cheaper, second-class coaches. It might be preferable, he added, to have separate cars but there was no necessity for such a step. There was no segregation on street cars, and at the hotels "the colored people are not received because their reception would interfere with the accom-

[10]Tindall, *South Carolina Negroes*, 68–73. Hampton quickly came under attack for failure to protect Negro rights. As an unsuccessful candidate for Congress, Colonel E. B. C. Cash of dueling fame charged Hampton with violating his pledges to South Carolina's colored citizens. Charleston *News and Courier*, September 4, 1882.

[11]Charleston *News and Courier*, April 2, 1885. Grady's article appeared in the April, 1885, issue of *Century Magazine;* Cable's was published in the January, 1885, issue of the same magazine.

modation and comfort of white people, especially the visitors from the North and East." [12]

Grady said the South would solve the race problem "with calmness and deliberation, without passion or prejudice." Dawson was not so sure. What if a split appeared in political ranks? "Suppose, for instance, that next year, or three years hence, there were Independent candidates for State offices in South Carolina, and these Independents were men of character and courage. The colored people, in large measure, would support the Independent candidates, and so, between the regular candidates and the Independents, the bidding for the colored votes would begin. Who shall say how far the bidding will go?" When Ben Tillman and his wool hat boys came along five years later, the political division which Dawson both predicted and feared occurred with a fury which left scars still visible on the South Carolina scene. And, irony of ironies, Ben's agrarian upstarts captured the Democratic party so completely that it was the conservative Old Guard which greedily eyed the Negro voter, *not* the new "Independents." [13]

The race issue erupted at the annual convention of the South Carolina Episcopal Church in 1887, and Colonel E. M. Seabrook was in the thick of the fight. That body adopted a ten-minute speaking rule so the colonel subsequently published a pamphlet entitled *The Law & the Gospel as Applied to the Questions before the Diocesan Convention of the Episcopal Church of the Diocese of South Carolina: The Race Issue Squarely Met.* Seabrook said denying a convention seat to a properly ordained delegate because his skin was not white was ridiculous and violated the legal canons of the Protestant Episcopal Church of America and the fundamental principles of Christianity.

I have heard it said that, if a colored clergyman is admitted to a seat in the Convention, it will lead to the social equality of the white and colored races. It must be confessed that when this is said by grown men, it is with difficulty that one's impatience is restrained. Social equality is governed by laws as fixed as the laws of gravitation. Since the origin

[12]*Ibid.*, April 3, 1885. This is an extensive two-part editorial entitled "In Plain Black and White."
[13]Dawson at first tried to cooperate with Ben Tillman, but soon he and the emerging rural demagogue were bitter enemies.

of man society has formed itself. People of like tastes, habits, and education associate together, and no laws make it otherwise. ' 'Tis the eye of childhood that fears the painted devil.' . . .

To make a *Christian Church a race Church* is to attempt to put back the hands of the clock of time over two thousand years and to get back to the period before the birth of Christ—*and this is the Nineteenth Century!* It cannot be done; it is an impossibility.[14]

Of course, it was done; in fact, it had *already* been done in the vast majority of American churches even as Seabrook wrote. If the colonel failed to convince some of his religious brethren of their fallacious reasoning, he at least influenced the thinking of his son. If by any chance he read Isaac's essay before he died in 1895, he must have been proud of the views it contained.

A strange "experiment" in racial discrimination in the fall of 1889 set the stage for repeal of South Carolina's civil rights statutes and saw the first of many Jim Crow bills dropped into the legislative hopper. Early in November, shortly before the state fair opened in Columbia, the Richmond and Danville Railroad announced that excursion trains to the fair would be segregated. The *News and Courier* commented: "This regulation shows a very obliging spirit on the part of the railroad authorities, and no doubt many ladies will in consequence come to the Fair who could not otherwise have attended. The plan proposed is to open only two coaches at a time while trains are being loaded, so that the conductors may easily direct the separate races to their separate cars." [15]

One week later, while commenting upon the deliberations of the Mississippi constitutional convention, the same newspaper took one of its strongest stands in favor of complete segregation. It scorned talk of suffrage restrictions and property qualifications for voters. Such steps, it said, would not solve the problem and, at best, would merely gain a brief respite from political troubles. ". . . the *News and Courier* believes, and has said over and over again, that the race question in this country can only be settled permanently, with regard to the best interests of *both* races, by the gradual but com-

[14] E. M. Seabrook, *The Law & the Gospel as Applied to the Questions before the Diocesan Convention of the Episcopal Church of the Diocese of South Carolina: The Race Issue Squarely Met* (Charleston, 1887), 13-15.
[15] Charleston *News and Courier*, November 7, 1889.

plete and final separation of the races. Why should we defer longer the adoption of the only mode of settlement which is certain of operation, and which, there is every reason to believe, we shall be compelled to adopt in the end?"[16]

One month later, repeal of Chapter CIX of South Carolina's *General Statutes*, "Of Offences Against Civil Rights," wiped out the last barrier to Jim Crow legislation and was in itself, if such were necessary, proof of the rising power of Tillman and his agrarian horde.[17] The vote on this measure is both interesting and baffling. It passed the lower house with little difficulty, but ran into a snag in the all-white senate and was defeated on December 20, 1889, by a vote of 15 to 14. The following day the senators agreed to reconsider repeal, and the bill eventually passed, 25 to 4.

This action was, in fact, in response to a direct appeal from Governor J. P. Richardson. Citing the recent "Jim Crow experiment," Richardson told legislators there was no good reason why such an arrangement should not be made permanent; and as a first step he suggested amendment of Chapter CIX to relieve common carriers from "the disabilities under which they have been placed by those who no longer represent the State, and [so] that a reform which is demanded by public sentiment may not be further impeded."[18] Richardson pointed out that intermixture of the races in coaches was frequently "attended by unpleasant incidents"; if facilities were equal, "there could be no objections by thoughtful persons of either race." A separate coach bill was introduced as the governor suggested, but it got bogged down in committee.

In a strange editorial appearing just as debate on Chapter CIX began, the *News and Courier* attacked the Springfield (Mass.) *Republican* for saying there was racial discrimination on the railroads of South Carolina. This was not true! However, James C. Hemphill, who became editor following Dawson's murder in March, 1889, quickly added that perhaps it should be. The Richmond and Danville experiment had proven so successful that it

[16]*Ibid.*, November 14, 1889.
[17]This chapter consisted of nine sections (2601–2609). See *The General Statutes and the Code of Civil Procedure of the State of South Carolina* (Columbia, 1882), 730–32.
[18]South Carolina *House Journal* (Columbia, 1889), 49.

should be widely adopted "for the very good reason that it is best for the whites and best for the blacks that they should be kept separate." [19]

Despite flaccid prose, the governor's proposal brought a violent outburst from at least one Negro community. In a lengthy letter appearing on the front page of the Columbia *Daily Register* (December 13, 1889) seven Negro churchmen and educators of Orangeburg said such ideas were "unworthy" of his excellency and of the South Carolina General Assembly. "Is it not enough that the two races are hopelessly separated in nearly all the higher relations of life already? Are you not content with separate places of public entertainment, separate places of public amusement, separate places of public instruction, and even separate places of public worship? Why, in the name of common sense, of common humanity, of the common high-bred sensitiveness of every decent person of every color, should you wish to force further unnatural separation even upon the thoroughfares of daily travel?"

After all, the state already had first- and second-class coaches. Wasn't virtual economic segregation enough? "The only motive we can possibly, but most reluctantly, assign is the desire to needlessly offend colored ladies and gentlemen who have always had sufficient funds and sufficient refinement to ride in the usual first-class coach. If this be the motive in reality, the sooner it is known that cultural respectability in others than Anglo-Saxons is at a permanent discount the better."

They had always supposed, wrote these colored leaders, that those who talked about "elevating" the Negro were sincere. Could it be that these same people wanted to erect a "Chinese wall of separation"? Did they wish to make an inferior caste out of respectable citizens? If so, they warned, "then we say, be very careful. You will thus pervert a class of citizens, who have always been models of law-abiding fidelity and discreet forbearance, into the bitterest opponents, the indignant defiers of this particular law(?)."

[19]Charleston *News and Courier*, December 6, 1889. Hemphill served as editor until 1910.

In December, 1889, not only state but also national leaders were addressing themselves to the race problem. Throughout that month Washington dispatches described in detail how members of the United States Senate were lending support to a "Back to Africa" movement. On December 16, after citing appropriate quotations from Jefferson, Lincoln, Grant, and President Benjamin Harrison, the Charleston *News and Courier* stated flatly that it was impossible for the two races to live together in harmony. Yet, this paper admitted that two very troublesome aspects of the matter must be considered: 1) What was the place of the mulatto in the race picture? He was a product of American life and perhaps should not be forced to go to Africa. 2) What about the educated Negro?

. . . those who think that the Negro is 'here to stay,' contented to remain a 'toiler' in the lower rounds of society, will find themselves confronted at an early day, with a new and most important phase of the problem. The Negro now leaving the schools will not submit to be represented by such unnatural leaders as have hitherto pretended to lead him and have run off with the spoils of office—yet, who, if we take as an example of their aspirations the greatest among them, would have every one cross the race line to form domestic ties. It is high time that both whites and blacks should understand that the men to represent the Negroes must be Negroes, with the instincts, sympathies, and self-interests of Negroes.

The *News and Courier* concluded that as the Negro increased his skills he would want to migrate to Africa and white Americans should help him on his way. It would be in "our" interest to do so. "It would be, it seems to us, a far-reaching economy to assist these people to enter a field suited to the widest employment and highest development of their energies. They would create new markets for American products, and in pushing the enterprises of America in the heart of the vast continent of Africa would reflect undying glories upon the land of their hard bondage and severe discipline." On the twenty-first when the crucial state civil rights statutes were repealed, the *News and Courier* barely noted the fact and even termed the legislative day a "dull" one. The Columbia *Daily Register* saw things differently and commented at length upon the event. This newspaper pointed out that state law had prohibited separation of the races in railroad coaches while the "Inter-State Commission" permitted it, and such separation "commends itself to the common sense of all but fanatics." To retain such statutes "in defiance of public sentiment here and everywhere else" would merely break down respect for law. "The clauses regarding restaurants and hotels were dead letters from the beginning. The effect of the repeal is to regulate all these vexed questions to the operation of the Fourteenth Amendment. That is all."

As Henry Grady lay dying on December 23, 1889, the *News and Courier*, commenting upon speeches in the United States Senate encouraging Negro emigration, printed a blunt, even brutal editorial entitled "Send Them Back To Africa."

There is general agreement among these Senators [M. C. Butler (S.C.), Randall L. Gibson (La.), John T. Morgan (Ala.)], and among other persons who have given the subject careful consideration, that the problem can be settled in one way only—by the absolute and final separation of the races. The question can be satisfactorily disposed of in no other way. While the removal of the Negroes from the South to the North and West would undoubtedly relieve the situation in the Southern States, it would only serve to postpone the final settlement of the question, and transfer to our Northern and Western neighbors the evils from which we have suffered, and which, in the spirit of Anglo-Saxon fellowship, we would not saddle on any other part of the country. . . .

Thus, it would seem that as the 1880's drew to a close the noose of legal segregation was beginning to tighten around the South Carolina Negro. The basic statutes on which federal and state civil rights legislation rested had been swept aside. An "experiment" in Jim Crow railway cars was hailed as a success, and bills seeking to make such an arrangement permanent were already appearing in the legislature. The South Carolina Negro did not yet—according to C. Vann Woodward and George B. Tindall—face formal discrimination at some bars, soda fountains, and theaters in urban centers such as Charleston and Columbia. Apparently he was not welcome at hotels and restaurants. There is, however, no evidence of residential segregation in larger communities. In rural areas the Negro usually did not even try to attend public functions, and probably had little interest in doing so. If admitted at all, he found himself relegated to stuffy balconies or rear sections.

These conditions were, of course, merely a reflection of custom. For generations the city slave and free Negro could be found in crowds attending public gatherings, in bars, at the theater, etc. A slave might be present in the service of his owner. In theory the status of both slave and free Negro was carefully regulated by state law and city ordinance; but, as Richard C. Wade makes clear in *Slavery in the Cities* (1964), urban life tended to strain, blur, and even disregard the printed word. A slave living in rural South Carolina faced a myriad of restrictions; for, with the rise of abolition and increasing fear of revolts, there had developed by the 1840's a system of surveillance not unlike that of South Africa today.[20]

An act passed in 1839 divided the state into districts to be patrolled at least once every fortnight to apprehend slaves not on their plantations. All white males between the ages of eighteen and forty-five were liable for duty. Unless a slave had a letter or ticket from his master he received a "moderate whipping" with a switch, not more than twenty lashes. The patrol could enter disorderly houses, vessels, and slave meetings. Also, a slave carrying a gun might be whipped unless accompanied by a white person over ten years of age. The act required each settled plantation to keep in residence at least one white man fit for patrol duty.

Another act passed five years earlier prohibited South Carolinians from teaching slaves to read and write. A white person who did so might be fined $100 and receive six months in jail; a free Negro, fifty lashes and a fine of $50. This same act also prohibited employment of slaves or free Negroes as clerks and salesmen. Whites who joined free Negroes, slaves, or mulattoes in any "game of chance" might get thirty-nine lashes and be imprisoned at the discretion of the court. If fined, one-half of the sum went to the informer; the other half, to the state.[21] A slave needed a permit from his master in order to sell goods to any storekeeper. A merchant found

[20] See John Belton O'Neall, *The Negro Law of South Carolina* (Columbia, 1848), and *The Militia and Patrol Laws of South Carolina to December, 1851* (Columbia, 1852), especially pp. 44–49.
[21] O'Neall, *Negro Law*, 46.

"trafficking" illegally with slaves faced a $1000 fine and up to twelve months in jail.[22]

To obtain liquor, slaves were supposed to have written orders from their owner. Liquor venders faced a $100 fine and up to six months in jail if apprehended selling without such permits. Again, one-half of the fine went to any informer; the other half, to the state. A system of patrols, written permits, informers, whippings, fines, and compulsory illiteracy is hardly the best preparation for citizenship; and, although the letter of the law was certainly not observed, these statutes undoubtedly had more influence in the countryside than in urban centers—*and*, nineteenth-century South Carolina was overwhelmingly "countryside."

In the last years of the Victorian Age, with a population of about a million and 60 per cent of those citizens colored, that state had a mere handful of communities which might be termed urban. In 1870 only Charleston (48,956) and Columbia (9,289) had more than 5,000 inhabitants, and the population of each was approximately 55 per cent Negro. The 1880 census returns revealed that Charleston and Columbia had about the same totals as in 1870, but Greenville now had 6,160 residents, having nearly tripled in size in a decade. Ten years later Spartanburg had 5,544 residents. Yet, in 1890 only these four communities had more than 5,000 inhabitants, and they contained only 8 per cent of the state's total population. Perhaps even more important, according to the 1890 census 18 per cent of South Carolina's whites and 40 per cent of her Negroes over ten years of age were illiterate.

With the arrival of Benjamin Ryan Tillman on the political scene it was apparent that, in time, the farmers' hero would seek a farmers' solution to race relations. To his host of agrarian faithful any

[22] In November, 1846, South Carolinians living in the Barnwell and Edgefield area became so distressed by illicit trade that they formed an association to boycott merchants suspected of such dealings. They said their slaves were stealing and selling produce, farm implements, their own allowances, and even taking clothes from the lines to trade for liquor. In a statement adopted on November 21, 1846, the members pointed out, "Such a state of things must speedily put an end to agriculture and Negro slavery. . . . Thus slavery becomes indeed a curse; one equally fatal to the master and the slave. And if the evils and dangers cannot be remedied, the sooner the whole system is eradicated the better for all concerned." *Preamble and Regulations of the Savannah River Anti-Slave Traffick Association* (n. p., 1846), 4–6.

racial intermingling which they saw in Charleston and Columbia was: 1) evidence of the moral decay of Wade Hampton's Bourbons, 2) a disgusting remnant of Black Reconstruction days—or, 3) perhaps a mixture of both! Nevertheless, the political turmoil which Tillman's election brought to South Carolina in 1890 caused legislators who were divided on so many issues to declare a tacit moratorium on racial matters. Each year a Jim Crow railroad bill appeared in the legislature, but got nowhere. In 1893 lawmakers passed an act permitting each taxpayer to designate when he paid his school tax which individual school in his district he wished to support; but, for the most part, state politicos were much too busy establishing colleges for farmers' sons and daughters, chastising corporations, and arguing over liquor laws to give much attention to Jim Crow.

In December, 1894, the annual separate coach bill was attacked in the house as merely an appeal to prejudice. It eventually passed by a close margin; but, as would happen for the next few years, the measure died in the senate. Within a few weeks, however, all that South Carolinians could talk about was the constitutional convention, the first in nearly three decades. The *News and Courier* appealed valiantly for unity among whites whose ranks had been shattered by the Tillman upheaval: "Let the convention be a white man's convention out and out, elected and supported by the white people of the State. We can trust the white man to do right by the inferior race, but we cannot trust the inferior race with power over the white man." [23]

The only issue, said Editor Hemphill, was *white supremacy*. When W. J. Rhees of Sumter County asked a question which was baffling many South Carolinians—how to disfranchise the Negro without taking the ballot from many whites—Hemphill told him what the state needed was a constitution which would "disfranchise as few white men and as many colored men as possible." When Rhees asked how loyal Negroes who had supported Hampton in the election of 1876 should be treated, Hemphill had a ready answer. Since these individuals had voted against the majority of their race in '76 for good government, they should be willing to sacrifice

[23] Charleston *News and Courier*, February 7, 1895.

their votes in '96 for good government once again. This editor even went so far as to endorse Tillmanites! If one had to choose between a Negro nominee (or one of his allies) and a Tillman supporter, swallow hard and vote for the latter.[24]

Ben Tillman, who had recently stepped down after two rip-snorting terms as governor, had his own ideas concerning the impending convention. Late in April, 1895, a Negro reporter who *sat* with him on a train trip from Augusta to Columbia asked the stern demagogue if delegates would attempt to cut Negro voting strength. Ben said yes, they most certainly would, but he wasn't sure just how it would be done. When the reporter asked why, Ben replied, "Well, we had a sample of what the Negro would do if he had power from 1868 to 1876, and that was enough; we don't want any more of it." [25]

A few weeks later Tillman granted an interview at his Trenton home to a colored preacher named Carroll from Ridge Springs. The preacher, who was *not* invited to come up on the porch and sit down as they chatted, concluded his report with these words: "I believe he has no ill feeling for the Negroes and would like to let them alone, but he is afraid that the dissatisfied faction will use the Negro to put his administration out of power, and he is working harder against white people than Negroes. Like A. Lincoln, 'If freeing the slaves will save the Union and stop the war, I am willing to do it.' So the freedom of the slaves was a 'war measure.' So with Governor Tillman. If disfranchising the Negroes will make him and his administration safe and sure, he is willing to do that or anything else." [26]

By the "dissatisfied faction," Preacher Carroll meant, of course, the conservative Old Guard whom Tillman and his followers over-threw in 1890. But if the line-up of delegates to the convention was a true indication of voter sentiment throughout South Carolina, Tillmanites had little to fear from their disorganized adversaries. Of 155 delegates, only 43 were conservatives.[27] When these men

24 *Ibid.*, March 14, 1895.
25 *Ibid.*, April 26, 1895, quoted in the Charleston *Enquirer.*
26 *Ibid.*, July 3, 1895. Carroll also talked with several Negroes who worked for Ben—among them was his mail boy. How did he like the senator? 'Putty well. But, oh he can cuss so! He cuss all de time!" "Cuss who?" "Everybody!"
27 Francis B. Simkins, *Pitchfork Ben Tillman, South Carolinian* (Baton Rouge, 1944), 289.

assembled on September 10, 1895, in the hall of the South Carolina house of representatives, there were numerous colored spectators in the galleries, six Negroes among the delegates themselves, and the rostrum was graced by a handsome bouquet sent by the Women's Rights Association—a group whose cause was as hopeless as that of the Negro. The delegates listened attentively as Governor John Gary Evans stressed the need for education and called for their earnest support. In commenting upon an educational qualification for voting, he remarked, "We mean no injustice to the Negro, but the reign of intelligence must be perpetuated." [28]

With preliminaries over, delegates got down to business; and sometimes tempers flared. Late in September, Colonel Robert Aldrich of Barnwell proposed to limit the house of representatives to white members. Tillman said no! The federal courts would strike down any such provision, and it might endanger the entire constitution. Aldrich suggested Ben was faint-hearted, or perhaps scared. "Not scared, Colonel," snapped Tillman, "but no fool!" The measure was tabled, 102 to 25. [29] Colored delegates said the main issue facing Tillman was how to keep the Negro from uniting with the conservative Democrats; and, in a letter to the New York *World*, five of six Negro delegates explained in great detail what was transpiring at Columbia. The 1890 census listed 132,949 Negroes and 102,567 whites of voting age in South Carolina, a Negro majority of 30,382. The census also revealed that of these potential voters 58,086 Negroes and 13,242 whites were illiterate. If an educational test were honestly administered, it would mean 89,325 white and 74,863 Negro voters, a white majority of 14,462.

But the nut for Tillman to crack is how he can disfranchise the Negro without disfranchising the 13,242 illiterate whites, whose votes would be lost entirely to his faction should the Conservative element nominate and vote an independent ticket. The highest vote his faction has been able to poll in round numbers is 60,000 and the Conservatives [,] 35,000. If Tillman's faction, therefore, should lose 13,242 votes it would leave him only 46,758 votes and the Conservatives 35,000 votes, and Tillman's majority over the Conservatives would be only 11,758 votes.

It will readily be seen that the 74,863 Negro votes or any considerable

[28] Charleston *News and Courier*, September 11, 1895.
[29] *Ibid.*, September 28, 1895.

part of them uniting with the Conservatives would make that faction master of the situation, and that is what Tillman wants to prevent. He has thus far hypnotized the whites of both factions with the scare crow, 'White Supremacy,' which he has shaken in their faces on every occasion, and which he is shrewd enough to know has the same effect upon the whites as a red flag upon an enraged bull.

The real truth is that 'White Supremacy' has never been endangered; for even in the days of Republican ascendancy all the great offices, and a large number of all the offices, were held by white men, and no one ever thought of making it a Negro government.[30]

At one point in mid-October the Charleston *News and Courier* suggested the convention might increase the white electorate by conferring suffrage upon South Carolina's women, but no one seemed interested in that idea. George D. Tillman, Ben's elder brother, caused a sensation when he attacked the provision on miscegenation as it came from committee. As written, the proposal would have prohibited intermarriage between whites and anyone with Negro blood. George, who was not on good terms with his more famous brother, said he knew of at least a hundred families in Aiken, Barnwell, Colleton, and Orangeburg counties who would be affected by such a sweeping measure, and some of them had proud Confederate veterans in their midst. There was, he claimed, "not a full-blooded Caucasian on the floor of this convention!" He forcefully reminded astonished delegates that all of them carried the blood of Mongolians, Arabs, Indians, and what-have-you in their veins. He moved that the section go back to committee and that the long accepted rule that a person with one-eighth Negro blood or less was legally white be restored. The convention agreed. Although George stopped just short of the obvious assertion he might have made, the *News and Courier* headlined its daily report from Columbia with words which left little doubt as to what the elder Tillman really meant: "ALL NIGGERS, MORE OR LESS!"[31]

Eventually, late in October, delegates got to the serious matter of suffrage. On the twenty-fifth Thomas E. Miller, who later

[30]*Ibid.*, October 3, 1895, quoted in the New York *World*. The calculations, at least as printed in the *News and Courier*, are somewhat in error and have been corrected. However, the totals are essentially the same.
[31]Charleston *News and Courier*, October 17, 1895.

became the first president of the state Negro college at Orangeburg, eloquently cited the long service his race had given to
South Carolina: "We are at the parting of the waves. The committee offers you white supremacy and white degradation. We offer
you the supremacy of law, of intelligence, and property." [32]

However, it was the man whom Ben Tillman once described as
"the ablest colored man I ever met" who presented the most compelling case for Negro rights.[33] William Whipper, also a delegate
to the 1868 convention, admitted the inferiority of his race. After
all, how could thirty years of education wipe out centuries of
illiteracy? "We are feeble in numbers in the country," he said,
"feeble in wealth, ignorant it may be true." But as whites climb
up the ladder of improvement, why not let the Negro use the
same ladder? "Don't pull it up after you!" Whipper criticized both
of the Tillmans for their repeated use of the word "nigger" on
the convention floor, and he added, "What I ask is that we be
treated as men and we will be [men]."

Then, turning to the proposed suffrage provisions, he said,

I appeal to you in your sovereignty, not to commit this wrong. God
in the plenitude of his wisdom will see this wrong corrected, and the
Negro will abide his time. The Negro is here and to stay and I warn
you to prepare to meet the issue. Only treat him fair. They are not
going away. They are needed here. You have too many uncultivated
fields. You have your forests awaiting the axeman to turn it [sic] into
money. Instead of trying to wipe out his political rights, it is your
duty to make him what he wants to be—your friend. You can trust
him now if you treat him fair and that's all he wants and demands.

What are the results of these wrongs? The Negro is wronged in
church and State. The doors of education are barred against him to
a large extent. What is the result? He goes to seed.

Here in his native land he is treated as an alien, an enemy. He is
lynched.

Whipper conceded no amount of oratory could change convention votes, but "sooner or later, God is right, and eventually
right will prevail. The consciousness that we are men makes us

[32] *Ibid.*, October 26, 1895.
[33] Quoted in Tindall, *South Carolina Negroes*, 81.

confident that our rights will eventually be protected." The Negro's interests, he warned the delegates, were really their own interests. He asked them to rise above prejudice and come up to a "liberal standard" in their work. "Do it in justice to the Negro, civilization, yourselves, and your posterity." [34]

Ben Tillman reacted to these speeches with a harsh attack upon both Whipper and Robert Smalls, the only Negro holdovers from Reconstruction days. He tried to prove they had been involved in all sorts of corruption, but his real task was to stave off revolt in his own ranks. Many of his followers were concerned that the new suffrage law would eliminate white voters as well as black. The proposed law, essentially the Mississippi Plan of 1890, provided that every male adult who fulfilled certain residence and tax requirements, who had not been convicted of specific crimes, and who could read or interpret any section of the new constitution when it was read to him could be enrolled as a lifetime voter up to January 1, 1898. After that date a registration board of "three discreet persons" appointed by the governor with approval of the senate would rule on an applicant's eligibility. Those facing these boards had to be able to both read and write any section of the constitution submitted to them. Ironically, after three-and-one-half pages of detailed legal jargon, the fifteenth and last section of the chapter on suffrage proclaimed, "No power, civil or military, shall at any time interfere to prevent the free exercise of the right of suffrage in this State."

It hardly seems necessary to point out the pitfalls which had been prepared for the Negro. The law skillfully skirted the legal language of the Fifteenth Amendment and established requirements which few Negroes, but most whites, could meet. It was approved on November 1, 1895, by a vote of 69 to 37, exclusive of pairing.[35] The next day Thomas Miller made this comment to a Columbia reporter: "Under this new Constitution or suffrage plan passed last night, the man who dreams of fair and honest elections is a fit

[34]Columbia *Daily Register*, October 27, 1895. The remarks of Robert Smalls, another Negro delegate, can be found in this issue.
[35]Charleston *News and Courier*, November 2, 1895. Two days earlier woman suffrage was defeated, 99 to 42.

subject for a place in a lunatic asylum and it will be a pity to turn him loose on the community." [36]

Early in December the convention came to a close, and on January 1, 1896, the constitution which it wrote became the law of South Carolina without ever having been submitted to the people for approval.[37] When the legislature convened a few days later, a Jim Crow railroad bill appeared. During the debate, one legislator argued that separation of the races was necessary since the railroad was "the only corporation that subjected the fair women of the state to the necessity of riding in a car with an inferior class." [38] Despite his views and those of a majority of house members, the senate rejected the bill.

Again in 1897, Bankston L. Caughman of Saluda—Red Shirt veteran of 1876, Alliance man, and pro-Tillman—introduced the annual Jim Crow measure. Although the railroad committee of the house returned an unfavorable report, members approved Caughman's bill, 80 to 18. Commenting on this wide margin, the Columbia *State* said, "The separate coach bill is not very accurately styled a 'jim crow car' measure, for it requires equal accommodations for whites and colored, which is not what the nickname suggests. The chief objection to the bill is that it is wanton, for there is no such condition of things as makes it necessary. We have never known a colored passenger in a first class car to be offensive in his bearing; and, if the point of attack were the misconduct of Negro passengers, an act empowering conductors to remove offenders to the second class coach would be ample for protection." [39]

[36] Columbia *Daily Register*, November 5, 1895.
[37] This constitution included an "anti-lynching" law which, interestingly, was the only such state law passed in the nineteenth century. Kentucky passed an anti-lynching act in 1920—Texas, in 1949. But, despite agitation for legislation, by mid-century these were the only states with such laws. See Pauli Murray, *States' Laws on Race and Color* (Cincinnati, 1950). The South Carolina law stated that if a prisoner were taken from officials and lynched, the officials were guilty of a misdemeanor and might be so charged. The country where a lynching occurred was liable for damages (not less than $2,000) to legal representatives of the person or persons lynched, and the county might recover any judgment from the parties committing the crime.
[38] Columbia *State*, February 6, 1896. This daily was founded in 1891 for the expressed purpose of opposing Ben Tillman.
[39] *Ibid.*, February 11, 1896.

As the senate prepared to tackle this measure, the *News and Courier* said, in a rather contradictory editorial, that if the bill passed the legislature it might be well to consider Jim Crow restaurants such as Georgia was establishing at railway stations.[40] "The suggestion is a good one," wrote Editor Hemphill. Yet, he could not really see the necessity for Jim Crow cars in the first place. White and colored citizens rode together in much smaller streetcars. They had gotten along for thirty years without such a law—why now?

> To speak plainly we need, as everybody knows, separate cars or apartments for rowdy or drunken white passengers far more than Jim Crow cars for colored passengers.
> In our view the Jim Crow car bill is unnecessary and uncalled for, and should be killed. It is not needed for the protection or comfort of the white people. It imposes a needless affront on respectable and well behaved colored people. It increases the burdens and troubles of the already over-burdened railroads without due course . . . . And, our opinion is that we have no more need for a Jim Crow car system this year than we had last year, and a great deal less than we had twenty or thirty years ago.[41]

Apparently the senators agreed with Hemphill, for on the day his words appeared they killed the measure without debate, 20 to 13. On February 27 the Columbia *State* praised the upper chamber for "adhering with considerable steadiness to its theoretical function of preventing ill-considered and radical legislation," citing as examples the Jim Crow bill and a measure which would have required trains to stop at all stations.

On January 12, 1898, Caughman once more introduced his Jim Crow bill in the house. Two weeks later the *News and Courier* again rose to the attack, observing in a bored tone that no session of the legislature seemed complete without this proposal. Hemphill, in much the same language as he had used the year before, said the bill was unnecessary and scornfully pointed out the absurdities which might result if this theory of complete separation were carried out. "We have Jim Crow churches, theatres, hotels, col-

[40] Georgia did not pass any state law relative to separation of the races in restaurants. Hemphill refers to ordinances at the local level.
[41] Charleston *News and Courier*, February 25, 1897.

leges, schools. It is proposed to establish Jim Crow cars, and Jim Crow boats, offices, etc., etc., would follow. Why not save ourselves all the future ingenuity and elaboration on this line by establishing two or three Jim Crow counties at once, and turning them over to our colored citizens for their especial and exclusive accommodation, reserving the others for ourselves, and with an honorable understanding that each race should 'shinny on its own side of the line' strictly, hereafter."

Up to this point in his editorial it would appear that Hemphill had reduced to a shambles the arguments of those backing the Jim Crow bill. But he added two final sentences which, like his approval of segregated depot restaurants in 1897, throw considerable doubt upon his true intent: *"It would be an excellent arrangement, for both races, on more than one account. We might try it."* [42]

It seems that the *News and Courier*, which had been a strong advocate of separation of the races for over a decade—even favoring a "Back to Africa" movement—now had reservations. Why? There are several explanations. A violent opponent of Tillman and his crowd, the Charleston paper hesitated to approve any measure which they proposed. Perhaps its editor shrank from the stark conditions which complete separation of the races would lead to. Perhaps his flippant conclusion was merely meant to be stinging sarcasm. Or perhaps the *News and Courier* was trying to do a bit of "fence straddling" in order to retain readers with conflicting views.

On February 4 Bankston Caughman rose in the house and demanded to know *why* his bill was not on the calendar. The speaker informed him it had been tabled, and another measure substituted for it. After some parliamentary confusion Caughman won out, and his bill was returned to the calendar. The following day Caughman attacked the substitute as just what the railroads wanted and noted scornfully that it provided for "coops and only one water closet." Eventually Caughman had his way, and his Jim Crow bill passed, 80 to 26. Among those voting with the majority was Ellison Durant Smith ("Cotton Ed"), a youthful member from Lynchburg. There were, however, those who still had misgivings.

[42] *Ibid.*, January 25, 1898. Italics mine.

R. A. Meares, a Ridgeway lawyer, thought the bill would "tend to strain the relationship between the races." [43] Meares was in such a dilemma that house members excused him from voting. As passed by the lower chamber the Caughman bill provided for separate compartments in first-class coaches and a fine of $300 to $500 for violations of these provisions, which would not apply to nurses attending patients or to emergency trains.

At a session held on the evening of February 14 the senators took up the measure which its own railroad committee had once more termed "unfavorable." The bill eventually passed by one vote on the crucial second reading, 19 to 18.[44] The following day it won approval on the third and final reading, 21 to 13.

The *News and Courier* deplored this action, saying it saw no good reason for such a law. South Carolina had no Jim Crow cars twenty years earlier when—in that newspaper's opinion—race prejudice was at its height. Why now? However, the Columbia *State*, although staunchly anti-Tillman, agreed that perhaps the separate coach bill was a good idea after all. As phrased, it would inflict minimum expense on the railroads.

Until this year we have contended against such legislation as has now been effected, but the complaints have been so many and so constant against the intermingling of the races on railway trains that we have not felt disposed to contest the matter at this session. The seeming humiliation put upon respectable colored people is to be regretted, but they suffer from the conduct of those of their race who have not appreciated the privileges which they have been accorded on the railroads in this State. The obstrusiveness and hardly-veiled insolence of many Negroes constantly offends ladies traveling—and that settles it.[45]

---

[43] *Ibid.*, February 6, 1898. The following day this daily tried to clear up some of the confusion concerning passage. Apparently, as the speaker said, the Caughman bill had been tabled and effectively killed, but upon the insistence of its sponsor it was placed on the calendar as an amendment to the substitute bill which came from the railroad committee and was more favorable to railroads. In debate the substitute bill was defeated and Caughman's measure won approval and went on to the senate.

[44] Geographically those in the majority came from upland counties (especially in the northwest quarter of the state) and from areas served by major rail lines. The Columbia *Register*, February 15, 1898, said that despite the close vote, "it is quite apparent that the majority of the people in the state favor the Caughman bill, or some other which embodies the same principle."

[45] Columbia *State*, February 16, 1898.

And "settled" it was for half a century. When the law went into effect on September 1, the *News and Courier* reported that the transition was made "almost without notice." First-class cars, it said, had been separated by compartments for some time; yet it would take the public several months to get used to these new rules. "A great many whites have sat in the portion assigned to the colored race and vice versa." [46] In this same issue the *News and Courier* noted that the races had been separated on Georgia trains for some years and the system seemed to work well; however, attempts to segregate Augusta's streetcars had proved "entirely impractical." [47]

Jim Crow had, for all practical purposes, come of age in the state of South Carolina. During the next three or four decades state laws and local ordinances added numerous innovations to this strict code of social behavior. In 1905 the legislature permitted segregation on streetcars outside of corporate limits. Cities themselves soon made similar provisions within their jurisdictions. The following year railroads were required to separate the races at depot restaurants. In a case heard in November, 1913 [Tucker vs. Blease *et al*] the state supreme court denied the petition of a Dillon County family whose wards of mixed blood had been suspended from a white school. The justices agreed the children were legally white, but upheld the local school board's action, adding that it might be in the "best interests" of all concerned if school officials provided a *third* system in such instances. Some of the most absurd bills were enacted in 1915–16 as legislators tried to effectively separate textile workers. White and colored could no longer work together, use the same entrances, exits, pay windows, stairways, or windows at the same time. Nor could they at any time "use the same lavatories, toilets, drinking water buckets, pails, cups, dippers, or glasses." For obvious reasons some of these restrictions did not apply to firemen in boiler rooms or to those hired to clean and

[46] Charleston *News and Courier*, September 2, 1898. It should be noted that the Jim Crow railroad bill applied *only* to first-class coaches. Second-class cars were not segregated, but two years later the state permitted railroads to abandon second-class service which, in effect, made all rail service segregated.

[47] Georgia segregated coach travel in 1891, sleeping cars in 1899. The following year Augusta, which had an extremely rigid pre-war code restricting "slaves and free persons of color," separated the races on street railways.

repair toilets and factory buildings. In 1917 traveling shows were required to provide separate entrances for both races, although there was no legal assurance patrons might not mingle once they got inside a tent or an enclosure. A 1924 act separated the races in billiard parlors and pool halls, and a 1934 law prohibited racial mixing at parks, recreation centers, and beaches in counties with cities having a population of more than 60,000.

Yet the most striking aspect of Jim Crow's mature years in South Carolina is not how many laws and regulations were passed in his behalf but *how very few!* Except for a handful of provisions relating to travel, education, and intermarriage, one hunts almost in vain for regulations requiring separation of the races in movie theatres, at public gatherings, in hospitals, hotels, and restaurants not connected with transportation.

True, the state legislature passed a law in 1915 permitting cities to provide "by reasonable and suitable ordinances for the segregation of the races in their respective municipalities"; but, only Greenville, a growing industrial community in the Piedmont, seems to have taken advantage of this measure.[48] As early as 1912 that city had ordinances prohibiting whites from entering colored cemeteries (and vice versa) except when attending funerals or on business. Negroes and whites could not eat "in the same room, at the same table, or at the same counter." Those seated or standing in streetcars were separated by race; and, if it were thought advisable, trolley lines could operate all-white or all-black cars.

Within the next two decades more ordinances "to provide for separation or segregation of the races" made their appearance. Greenville city fathers even attempted to establish white and black blocks. Negroes could not move into a block where whites were in a majority, nor whites into a block where Negroes predominated— if the majority objected. And even if no objections were voiced, whenever a block became all-white or all-black its status was frozen. These residential restrictions did not apply to domestics living in quarters provided by their employers.

By 1953 several more refinements had been added to a code which

---

[48] Some South Carolina cities, Rock Hill among them, merely reproduced the state law of 1915 in their codes as a warning that local ordinances would appear should need for them arise.

already included a dozen specific regulations relating to racial mixing. Among these was a ban prohibiting the two races from occupying the same compartment in a taxicab. In that same year, on the eve of the U.S. Supreme Court decision relating to segregated schools, Greenville passed perhaps its most ridiculous ordinance. City fathers decided that, after all, Negroes and whites *could* eat in the same room if that room were very, very large! Serving areas had to be at least thirty-five feet apart, and the intervening space occupied by merchandise, display cases, or something of that sort. Such establishments were to have separate tables, booths, or counters, and separate utensils marked "by some appropriate color scheme or otherwise;" and, these separate utensils were to be cleaned in separate facilities. As late as 1956 Greenville was doggedly strengthening its racial barriers; but, not too surprisingly, all such regulations are missing from the 1964 edition of that city's code.[49]

Of course, absence of specific laws and ordinances at either the state or local level does not mean Jim Crow did not have a flourishing career in South Carolina from the 1870's to almost the present day. He was extremely healthy, for a rural society with its strong adherence to custom, tradition, or whatever one wishes to call it kept him so. Most towns and cities did not find it necessary to enact regulations of any kind. Greenville, with a relatively small Negro population (40 per cent) and a constant influx of white mill workers from rural counties, seems to be the lone exception.

As this survey of racial laws and Isaac DuBose Seabrook's essay indicate, Jim Crow's career was not as strange in South Carolina as it may have been in some parts of our nation. C. Vann Woodward's *Strange Career of Jim Crow* emphasizes that: 1) stern legal

---

[49] It is interesting to note that at the very time the Greenville city council was strengthening racial barriers, a city-county community organization was conducting a sweeping survey of Negro facilities. This study—by turns reactionary, liberal, and even daring—was published as *Everybody's Business* in 1950. The report called for increased educational and vocational opportunities for Negroes, but at the same time asked the local bus company to demand strict adherence to state law so as to prevent standing in the aisles. Interestingly enough, Negroes themselves saw *apathy* as their greatest problem. Low income groups seemed satisfied with their lot, and upper income levels had no idea (according to this survey) of what they might do to help improve conditions among their race.

segregation has not always been the way of life in the South; 2) there was a bright time—a "Camelot" circa 1875–90—when some Negroes and whites were associating freely (as they had for decades) and *all* blacks were not treated as an inferior caste; and, 3) in those halcyon days three alternatives to legal segregation existed: liberal, radical, and conservative approaches to race relations. Needless to say, the liberal philosophy of a man such as George Washington Cable attracted virtually no South Carolinian. The radical approach developed by the Populists in the 1890's ("We're all poor farmers being exploited by city corporations, so let's work together for our common good.") also had little chance in that state. Ben Tillman and his followers, strongly imbued with Populist ideals, captured the machinery of the Democratic party so completely that there was no necessity for them to cooperate with either the Negro or the Old Bourbon whom they routed, especially after they rewrote the state constitution so as to perpetuate their power.

The conservative approach, on the other hand, was tried in South Carolina. General Wade Hampton as governor from 1877 to 1879 is an excellent example of that philosophy in action. The essence of Hampton's attitude was that of a kindly, responsible aristocrat concerned for the welfare of a hard-working ex-slave. Hampton and his sort attempted to chart a middle course between extremist factions. As Woodward describes them: "The conservatives acknowledged that the Negro belonged to a subordinate role, but denied that subordinates had to be ostracized; they believed that the Negro was inferior, but denied that it followed that inferiors must be segregated or publicly humiliated. Negro degradation was not a necessary corollary of white supremacy in the conservative philosophy." [50]

Despite the prestige of his name and his exploits in the Civil War, Hampton was unable to make South Carolina adopt his views. Even many of his close political associates fought all efforts to put this conservative philosophy into practice, and the general must have uttered a sigh of relief when he relinquished the post of governor in 1879 and headed for the United States Senate.

[50]C. Vann Woodward, *The Strange Career of Jim Crow* (New York, 1966), 48. This is the second revised edition of the Richards Lectures delivered at the University of Virginia, originally published in 1955.

In *After Slavery: The Negro in South Carolina, 1865–1877,* Joel Williamson questions this traditional picture of Hampton as a benign aristocrat, eager but unable to chart a reasonable course in race relations. He sees the general offering the Negro the privilege of voting for his ticket and nothing more. Hampton was, he concludes, "in perfect harmony with those native whites who steadfastly refused to recognize the Negro's political equality by joining with him in any political partnership."[51] Writing in 1949, some sixteen years before Williamson's study appeared, Hampton M. Jarrell eloquently detailed the more familiar story. In fact, the title of his work expresses its central theme—*Wade Hampton and the Negro: The Road Not Taken.*[52] As for the disputed election of 1876, both authors agree it was a quiet affair with evidence of some fraud. However, Williamson tends to emphasize Hampton's *private* expressions to friends while he was seeking and holding public office; Jarrell emphasizes the general's public utterances. Whatever Wade Hampton's true intent, with his departure for Washington there was no local figure strong enough to oppose the rural forces which soon emerged under the Tillman banner.

It would be wrong to assume that every Tillmanite was a rank Negrophobe or that each Jim Crow law was impelled by unreasoning hatred for the black man. Other factors—a desire to put the railroads in their place, a belief in the "God-given" right to remake South Carolina society in the image of a small Calvinistic county seat, a yearning to conform to practices in neighboring states, and a strong urge to "get even" with Low Country aristocrats who for generations had been running roughshod over the wishes of Up Country farmers—all of these are evident in the Jim Crow movement. And it would be equally incorrect to presume that those opposing Jim Crow were always expressing concern for the plight of the Negro. Frequently those voicing such opinions were merely pro-railroad, anti-Tillman diehards who (like the Charleston *News and Courier*) had been advocating complete separation of the races prior to 1890.

Also, to some degree the Negro himself is to blame for trends evident in South Carolina in the late nineteenth century. On the

[51]Williamson, 406.
[52](Columbia, 1949).

heels of Appomattox he was caught up in conflicting emotions. One way to reject slavery and all it stood for was to reject *in toto* the white race, set up a separate society, separate churches, separate schools. Yet, by taking such an independent course—while one may understand and sympathize with the motives—the Negro was removing himself from those influences he wished to emulate and imitate, i.e., the world of the Southern white. During Reconstruction years the Negro's attempts to bridge this gulf in any meaningful way met with rebuff and insult, only increasing the tendency to withdraw from such embarrassing contracts.[53] After 1877 this sometimes vague emotional and cultural barrier began to take on clear, precise, legal meaning.

One of the ironies of this sad tale is that, in effect, the Southern aristocrat was thrust from political leadership at the right moment. Had he remained in power in the 1890's the onus of Jim Crow would have fallen upon his shoulders. Instead, he stepped (or was pushed) aside, and his red neck, Up Country cousin did exactly what he would ultimately have done himself. But, the aristocrat of today is free to protest the innocence of his class. His hands are clean. His grandfather could even vote against Jim Crow measures in the state legislature, knowing they would pass and become law anyway. In effect, the red neck has been "used" once more. The twentieth century points an accusing finger at him as lynch-prone, depraved, the man who riveted stern segregation on the nation and made a travesty of our democratic heritage. Meanwhile, his white suit as clean as ever and his chivalrous reputation virtually intact, the aristocrat stands aloof and confident. With mock sincerity he deplores the deterioration of race relations. If talking with a fellow Southerner, he blames outside (Yankee) influences. If his conversation happens to be with those outsiders, he points to the revolt of the hill folk and thus attempts to absolve himself and his class of all responsibility.

It is not, however, that simple. If as banker, storekeeper, landowner, or lawyer he had stood up and spoken out many a lynching would not have taken place. But since he did not, there was created in his mind and in the minds of many other Americans—admit it or not—what Gunnar Myrdal calls the "American Dilemma." By

[53]See Williamson, *After Slavery*, 274–99.

this Myrdal means the "ever-raging" conflict between the "American Creed" which talks of high national and Christian precepts on one hand and community and group practices (prejudice, conformity, economic and social jealousies) on the other.[54] The all-white South Carolina senate which in 1889 voted 15 to 14 against repeal of that state's civil rights statutes knew this dilemma. So did the Ridgeway lawyer whom the house excused from voting on the Jim Crow railroad bill of 1898 and so did those senators who reluctantly passed it, 19 to 18. This same dilemma was, of course, real indeed to Isaac DuBose Seabrook. Were it otherwise, the essay which follows would not have been written.

Seabrook, looking at race relations in 1895, is clearly an exponent of what C. Vann Woodward calls the "conservative" approach.[55] Scattered freely throughout these pages is the concern of the old master for his ex-slave, portrayal of slavery as a "training school" for the rough African immigrant, and the nostalgic picture of a cavalier South peopled with happy blacks, benevolent whites, and vast plantations—a world which Seabrook (born in 1855) could hardly remember. Yet, at the same time, he recognizes the mounting economic competition of Negro and white workers, the Negro's innate distrust of "white man's law," and the chaotic conditions prevalent in many black households.

In the light of present-day scholarship some of his statements seem naive, but we are dealing here with a man caught up in—again I use the word—a dilemma. Seabrook owes considerable intellectual debt to the Old South, Charles Darwin, Hinton R. Helper, and scores of writers who in the 1880's and 1890's were trumpeting the worldwide triumph of the Anglo-Saxon. He brings together in a unique fashion many of the forces evident in the South in the last years of the nineteenth century. He has read and weighed the arguments of liberals such as Cable, has seen the Populist-Republican-Negro coalition take over in North Carolina, and is experiencing (even as he writes) Ben Tillman's "solution" to racial problems.

One can imagine this tall, attractive man—as hotel clerk, raconteur,

[54]Myrdal, *An American Dilemma* (New York, 1962), lxxxi. This is the twentieth anniversary edition of this profound analysis of racial attitudes and practices which first appeared in 1944.
[55]See his *Strange Career of Jim Crow*, especially 44–59.

gentleman of uncertain leisure—talking long and earnestly about the Negro's place in society. He and his friends probably spent many hours on The Battery chatting, discussing, arguing, and gazing across the water toward the low, gray outline of Fort Sumter. They were perhaps joined from time to time by colored acquaintances whose views may well be included in this essay. Undoubtedly such gatherings ended with a certain degree of frustration, mutual laughter, and uniform damnation of Benjamin Ryan Tillman. Then, symbolically, the whites went their way and the Negroes, theirs.

It was no doubt out of conversations such as these, out of studies at the University of the South and experiences in Charleston as worker, reader, and observer of the daily scene that Seabrook has fashioned his thesis. Whether he ever dreamed of publishing it is not known; but, with the trend of the times and lacking financial resources, publication became increasingly impossible. Now, thanks to the passage of some seventy years and especially to changes which have occurred during the past two decades in both historical scholarship and in our own society, Isaac DuBose Seabrook's analysis of race relations in 1895 can be better appreciated. And perhaps it may shed additional light upon a tortured episode in our national past.

Introductory

Natural causes are constant in their operation. So true is this generalization that the question as to what a thing is today involves the question as to what it was yesterday. Human beings as links in the great chain of cause and result are subject to the same law. For our science has passed that period of its infancy when man was regarded as something distinct from nature and superior to her methods.

So far as history gives any account, the Negro races of Africa, especially those utilized hitherto as slaves, have been in a condition of subjection either to native kings of despotic power or to neighboring tribes who captured and held them in a servile condition.

This leads us to a further and very important reflection which would appear absurd were it not so very true: namely this, that the white races of Europe never really enslaved the blacks, for in kidnapping and buying them and transporting them hither and thither about the world, they generally did little more than retain them in the condition of subjection in which they found them at home. Their condition of slavery was unaltered: the only change was one of masters; a change from the lifetime control of a savage, irresponsible ruler to that of a ruler irresponsible indeed, but less savage; involving also the further change from a servitude both ignorant and indolent, from which no progress was possible, to a servitude where some intelligence and industry were needful and from which improvement of race was a natural consequence.[1]

However, in either case, servitude in one form or another has been the fixed condition of life of the race. Two classes of results have followed from this state of things. The Negroes, by the effect of long tradition and habits transmitted through long periods of time while their race was yet under the African despot and further by the after effect of their subjection to the whites in the United States, acquired as a trait of mind—one may say a trait of the body itself, a very habit of the nerves—that disposition of ready submission which sprung of the conditions under which their race had so long lived. And, the second class of results was as follows: while becoming thus fixed in those traits that peculiarly belong to the slave, they further acquired from the whites certain habits of industry of a peaceable nature and such as suited not the future possibility of freedom, but their condition as slaves. Thus, both in the traits they inherited and in those they acquired, were they developed, shaped on the very form and mould of peaceable subjection. And such, the long continued slavery agitations and finally the war of 1861 found them; not restless, not active in their own behalf, not revengeful, not insurrectionary, but quietly pursuing their accustomed tasks and patiently and cunningly awaiting results, true to the inherited traits of a thousand years and ruled by habits and feelings, the birth of which lay buried in the sands and forests of Africa. And such, with some slight modifications, due to change of conditions, have they remained to the present day: a living example of the deliberate slowness by which the processes of nature unfold themselves.

Now let us mark a contrast. This race, which may be called the offspring of slavery, has been associated in this country with a race which has followed the very opposite course from a time

[1] Although in these pages Seabrook paints a much too attractive picture of American slavery, it is true that slavery has long been characteristic of African life. However, a slave was held usually only for a fixed period of time. Other cultures, Islamic and European, introduced the concept of a perpetual, lifetime, inherited slave status. See Donald L. Wiedner, *A History of Africa South of the Sahara* (New York, 1964), 45–70.

quite immemorial. From whatever root originally sprung, the Indo-Germanic races through their barbaric strength and vast numbers gradually seized upon and held the upper and middle parts of Europe: overrunning these and not resting content in the arts of peace, but still aflame with love of conquest and passion of war, they turned again and again, despite frequent repulses, their greedy eyes toward the sunny plains of Italy and the South, and thrust out ever and anon their savage arms to clutch the Roman world until at last these races came under the influence of the Roman Empire, that immense engine for the spread of civilization by force. But these barbarians after centuries of national friction, war, and tumult were destined to become the victors, not the slaves of their Roman foes. These rude Northern hordes full of that fresh strength that distinguished them by the side of the failing youth of the Romans acquired of them all the most valuable things which they could give: their arts, their sciences, their methods of warfare, and their laws, and gradually their religion, and turned them to their own use and to the building up of their own race destinies; while the Roman world, grown old and weak and having reached its climax and borne its fruit, faded away as the chief factor in the destiny of the world.

Henceforward, after the fifth century the history of Europe becomes one not of continued conquests of the Roman arms, but of the growth of its Northern races, helped forward not only by those traits of activity and strength developed in their long barbaric struggle with each other, but assisted also by the civilization they had gained, the mental and moral spoils they had won from their more civilized enemies of the South. Another branch of the same family, the English, in the fifth century and after them their near relatives, the Saxons, shewed more markedly the same greedy and strong traits and, seizing upon Britain, expelled and slew the former inhabitants and destroyed the results of the old Roman occupancy. Unlike the more easily tamed Germans, these English and Saxons, pirates and freebooters from Sleswick [*sic*] and Holstein, were never at any time subject to Roman influences, and their native strength, barbarism, and greed had then a fair field in which to develope themselves unchecked by the civilizing tendencies of Roman culture.

Those Europeans, largely descendants of the Anglo-Saxon branch who settled this country, have followed out the habits and obeyed the traits of their fathers. A little band of them has seized upon a new continent as the field of future operations. On the one hand they have driven away the native people, the Indians, who opposed their progress, offering them no compromises except those impossible to them; and, on the other, they have brought from the further side of the world to do their bidding a race gentle, yielding, submissive, and sprung from the very cradle of slavery itself, thus shewing in every way the same traits of energy, love of power, and grasping selfishness that have marked their path in history.

In the preceding pages I have aimed to sketch in general outline the history of the Negro race and to place by its side the history of the white race. I wished to emphasize the causes and the course of life which have made the Negro what he is and the causes and the course of life which have made the white man what he is. From this survey we see that the Negro has been reared in the school of slavery and has all the habits of the slave, and conversely that the white man has grown in the school of struggle and conquest and has the habits of aggression and domination. Thus are the two races the antipodes of each other, not only in superficial differences, but in the more radical differences of mental traits and inherited instincts, and each retains the heritage of the past whether it will or no.

From this tyranny of natural laws there is no escape; and a modification of their action, altho' possible under changed conditions, is so slow and goes on with so gradual a step, that resulting changes are scarsely perceptible in the lifetime of a generation of either race.

But we cannot stop here. If it be true that precedent causes are so potent in the history and present conditions of a race, it follows that if in any way these causes are themselves modified or other causes introduced there must be a corresponding modification in the results. If the two races now living together in this country—or either of them as has lately happened—is subjected to a different set of conditions from those hitherto existing, there must result at some time a corresponding change in the relations of these races; and, we shall find as we proceed that such is, in some measure, actually the case. We shall see that the African, though largely an African still, is becoming American; and that the slave, though not yet free of the habit of subjection, is gaining somewhat of the consciousness of freedom. The consideration of the two races in the aspects of their present relation as sprung from past causes and their future relation as sprung from modifications of those causes now at work forms the subject of the following chapters.

1

Looking   Backward

Landed property at the South took the shape of large estates. This was the natural condition of a newly and rapidly settled country, and the results which came of this were striking and important. The fact is that in the true sense of the word the Southern country had no population, except the comparatively few land owners scattered here and there at long intervals from each other. Besides these there was no class of people who were attached to the soil either by law or birth, or who felt that their well-being was bound up with it: not even a class of serfs, as in ancient Europe, who were a part of the land and who could only be sold with the sale of the land and whose interest, small as it was, to that extent was really centred in the soil of their birth.

The Negro multitudes who lived about these estates could have and had no possible interest in the lands upon which they existed; they could be moved by their masters from one estate to another at will and be sold away from the place of their birth at any time and sent in any quarter. For them, the tillers, the soil—however poor or however productive—could yield nothing more than the bare means of a simple existence. Thus, from their standpoint, they owed the soil nothing in the way of improvement. To their masters they yielded an amount of labor under a sort of compulsion. Having no interest in the lands and no motive in doing skilled work, the kind of work remained as poor and the amount remained as small as possible under the circumstances.

And so things stood, with a strong tendency to grow worse with the increase of the number of slaves for two hundred years: the population consisting of three or four hundred thousand slave owners and three or four million slaves whose individuality was obliterated, who had not interest in lands, nor towns, nor trades, nor arts; and lastly of the poorer non-slave-holding whites, who held small tracts of poorer lands, who were not profitably employed owing to the absence of varied industries which resulted from the slavery system. And from the same system and the accompanying method of tillage there sprung up for the South a full crop of evil consequences that finally cost the South more in material advance and in peace than could be cancelled by the value of the indigo, rice, and cotton—plus the value of the slaves themselves—produced under this destructive method.

The value of lands under this tillage and in the absence of emigration stood relatively stationary while that of lands in the "free states" doubled and trebbled itself. The hordes of Negroes toiling for no benefit to themselves and stirred by no ambition were still further held in their condition of ignorance and incompetence by laws designed to prevent their mental growth and which shut up to them the elementary knowledge of reading and writing. The element of intelligence was eliminated from their occupation. Thus like the lands upon which they lived, the tillers were also unimproved, and the conditions needful for a wealth-producing and thriving populace were absent. Thus the land had no skilled labor; and, as to emigration, it did not exist even in name.

But this discouragement of intelligence and absence of skilled workers produced commercial losses also. It became necessary that all implements of husbandry, all tools, all manufactured articles should be purchased elsewhere and imported into this Section, thus sending money away and leaving unemployed the home people, giving what would otherwise have been their legitimate wages to the skilled artisans and manufacturers of England or the North. The slow growth of cities and towns was another natural result of the system; for, where the active population was largely confined to the country and the other departments of work were so small in number and variety, the centres of such work were necessarily few and devoid of vitality. Thus a flourishing and diversified trade was impossible. Such were some of the material costs of the system of wide, undeveloped lands and tillage by ignorant, unpaid labor.

But the evils of the method were farther reaching. It exercised a very unhappy effect upon the morals of the white population. It modified profoundly and unconsciously their whole attitude toward life and their relations to each other. A marked antagonism arose between the slave-owning class and the free white laborer. Even within the limits of a single state these two radically distinct modes of life could not coexist peaceably. The state tended to become divided into the sections of the slave owner and the white farmer, into upper and lower Country; and a feud more or less defined existed between the two. The slave owner, feeling that his safety depended on his dominating the state, struggled for political control and all places of power and influence. This result they generally achieved, and the states were ruled by them, for and in their interest, the whole power of which they then wielded in a long, continued effort to control the General Government and the "free states" of the North and West.

An unconquerable pride grew up in the hearts of this class—the pride of unchallenged domination, of irresponsible control of others, of unquestioned power, of uncriticized conduct. Each man became a lord within his own domain. He was the source of law among his slaves; and his self interest and good or ill will was the rule of his actions: the laws of the state did not readily reach him and public opinion among his own class naturally coincided with his views. There thus resulted an absolute indifference to the opinions of others: an entire independence of the objects, needs, or aims of the other classes of the population. And this attitude of pride, of absolutism, extended itself beyond the limits of the plantation which had given it birth. The free white working people of the state were made to feel the power of irresponsible rule; they too must bow beneath the absolutism of the slave oligarchy. They indeed were being ruined by the success of the slaveholders. They were thus the enemies of the oligarchs. But of small avail could their enmity be. They possessed not the means nor organization to offer an effective opposition to the small class of autocrats who had seized upon society and the state.

In this state of things the sense of justice, of consideration for the fair claims of all, weakened and died out among a class whose daily occupation consisted in taking the fruits of others' toil without wages or recompense of an adequate sort; and, as a natural result, this habit of mind still clung to them not only in their dealings with their slaves, but in their dealings with each other and with other and less favored classes of the people. So that the mercantile, the farming, even the professional classes, and the teachers of youth must not be permitted to enter the favored heaven of the slave-holding aristocracy. They were at best useful servants; but in other respects, beings of another race, of a different world! They could have no claims upon "Society" in the only important sense of the word and must be grateful for the good will and condescension of their superiors. Particularly was the white artisan class to be treated with bare tolerance. This class was, by its very condition, hostile to slavery, for what did this class represent? It stood in the midst of slavery the champion of the free man's toil demanding pay for its work, demanding more than the mere right to live, demanding justice and fair dealing and consideration for man by man. It stood as the champion, albeit unsuccessful, of that pitiably situated class known as "the poor whites" and by the Negroes called "poor Buckra," a word of contempt and social damnation.

A step further must we pursue this melancholy subject, this sad and costly attempt to build up a state without a real population: this subjugation of the many and the ruin of most in order that a favored few may remain uncompromising rulers. In order that he may remain safe in his place of power, the despot demands that the subject shall live unconscious of his degradation, that not only his body be bound in chains, but that his mind shall remain in darkness, that all sense of individuality be taken away. Education he must not have. Intelligence, whatever its value to others, he must not possess; it is not one of his virtues, although it may assist the toil of the worker it also shews him his real condition and the condition of others more happily circumstanced and may illumine the path to betterment. It may bring unrest, disquietude into his mind hitherto enchained and endungeoned. By its help, be it never so feeble, the eager eyes of the prisoner may see beyond the gratings of his cell and find a road of escape or of safety.

Thus education came to be regarded as not very useful and certainly dangerous, as a luxury unfitted for the worker of any class, an apt cause of discontent, a fertile source of disaffection among any except the dominating few. So that among the blacks the school teacher was not to be thought of; and, for the same general causes, he was not vigorously encouraged among the whites. Polytechnic schools and agricultural colleges and all those intelligent means of improvement by which a people may advance their means of livelihood and vary their toil with benefit both to themselves, their employees, and their neighborhood found little place at the South: they did not suit its ideas, its methods of work, its social distinctions, and hence failed to receive efficient encouragement in that section. Chained in body and mind to the car of oligarchy, the entire people, black and white, followed perforce in its path, had its noise in their ears, and its dust in their eyes, held by its overgrown power ever behind and in subjection. Presently the triumphal car was converted into a chariot of war and then its captives, mainly those of the white race, were summoned to do its fighting and spend their pent up strength and use their blind force to perpetuate its power and their own bondage.

It seems to be generally supposed and in fact was really believed by the Southern people themselves that theirs was an industrial section engaged in agriculture, inhabited by peaceful Negroes, happily free from a turbulent white population, and entirely devoted to the arts of peace. And yet, from the standpoint of 1895, looking backward and assisted by the light of after results, we see distinctly that such was not the case. The condition of the South was not one of peace; it was not in a state of industrial repose. On the contrary, it was in a highly militant condition. War, although not present in act, was present in thought and hung on the horizon. Preeminently it was a Section. Its growth, its way of life, its system of slave labor, against which all the world had taken arms—as well as the North and West—made it a section and tended further and further to segregate it from the rest of the Union. Its real condition was one of strenuous antagonism. This antagonism was exerted in two directions, against two foes. Its oligarchy had been nurtured in the school of a resolute and militant opposition. At home their energy and force had been directed toward the control of large masses of slaves and as a consequence also to the control of their state governments and white populations.

But they had another and far stronger opponent to meet and subdue. This was none other than the General Government and the Free States. The struggle had been long and well defined; it was radical; it affected first principles; it was co-eval with the Constitution, nay, it antedated even that early Compromise. An armed truce had existed for near one hundred years; but, under this thin cloak of peace and union the causes of contest were alive and grew with the growth of the South and the more rapidly increasing power of North and West.

The days of the Old Revolution lay now far in the distance, and with them had passed somewhat into oblivion the feelings that then held sway. Men change and therefore political constitutions, however good, cannot remain fixed. Nations grow to manhood, and the swaddling bonds of their infancy are unconsciously laid aside, and that by degrees so gradual that the change is hardly seen. The letter of the Constitution indeed remained, but the mind of the people had outgrown it. "Esto perpetua" is a hopeful saying, but it remains true that no wisdom is prophetic enough to make perpetual laws for the distant future with new aims, new interests, and new needs. Human destiny, the laws of progress, the gusts of interest and passion laugh at human laws, forget them, and pass them by in silent neglect, or forcibly cast them off like useless clothes. From every page of history the great world spirit speaks of motion, of struggle, of endeavor. Form after form appears, ever new, ever changing, and dying leave their effects to those that follow. A vast panorama of which one sees one part, one another, but the great artist remains behind the scenes, the object of eternal worship and eternal ignorance!

And so it happened in the Western World as it slowly emerged from its uncertain youth into fuller manhood and clearer light. Full of fresh energy, the American people turned its steps Westward until the waves of the Pacific sounded in its eager ears.

The course of this Nation, for such it was fast becoming, was hemmed in by no iron band of foes: no hostile rivalry girded it about, ever on the watch to oppose and destroy. And, in this absence of foes, the need of close mutual protection tended to disappear, and died too that feeling of fraternal union so strong in the days of 1789. The new World to the Westward was arising with an ease and rapidity never before seen: a world of great hopes, of great wealth, of great extent. Easy before, the means of life became still easier, wealth more certain, the rewards of toil more sure. And there, as a natural result, content with the Government grew apace with the blessings it held out; and these blessings were open alike to the labor and skill of all sections—the North, the South, and the West.

But in the eager race for wealth, it gradually became apparent that the racers were no longer friends, but hostile competitors. It could not be denied nor hidden, the soft blandishments of rhetoric could not cover it, nor wishes for good will and peace conceal the fact of the contest. The North and West had grown by means of free toil and free exertion, by individual enterprise and individual intelligence. The South, by means of African slavery. They were no longer one: the line of difference was struck clearly and inevitably. The race, formerly one among citizens of a common country, now became one among foes for power. The North, now called a distinct section and felt to be cut off from the South, stood for further extension of free soil and free labor. The South, feeling herself also a distinct section, struggled for the extension and protection of slavery, saw in the threatened destruction of slavery the ruin of her interests, and heard in every voice raised against her the sound of doom. Thus in the natural course of things were the sections divided and that by no superficial distinction.

Slavery in the old Revolutionary epoch was common to both North and South, but in progress of time it gravitated Southward and grew in the more congenial clime of that section where the steaming fields and tropical air fostered its growth. In early days, as is well-known, it was regarded by both State and Church as an evil, but as time went on and it became a source of wealth and political power, men's minds at the South reversed themselves in obedience to their interests, its oft admitted evils were forgotten by convenient memories, and it was finally held to be a blessing. It had become enwrapped with the life of the Southern people. It had created a class of feudal barons who had no need of arms, but ruled the most plastic of serfs. It had nursed a lofty pride and an intolerance easily born in those whose word is law. It created a race of politicians in its defence, for the existence of slavery began now to depend on the successful management of the Government. It created good leaders and blind followers.

But, it stood in direct hostility to free white labor and must resist the power of the free North and the fresh strength of the rising West, and none knew this better than its advocates. Gradually and surely the forces collected themselves. The moral, social, and political world arrayed themselves against it. The Christian orator, the statesman, the poet, the workman armed themselves. They had before them the example of foreign nations whose voice had recently been given against slavery. In 1835, the opposition, long dormant, became aroused and resolved, but announced itself to be moral, not political in its aims and methods. A gust of anti-slavery writings, pamphlets, and tracts was blown over the land. Paid lecturers spoke against it in public. Pulpits thundered anathemas; excited women and those whose feelings are easily aroused on all subjects—fanatics, well meaning but ignorant—burned with righteous rage against the Southern despots and drivers. Politicians spoke of Southern "plantation manners" and haughtiness in Congress. Across the Atlantic the same cry arose where a preacher of the Gospel of Charity denounced the Southern states as "brothels." It may be supposed that in this sulphurous air the imagination of people became unhealthily aroused.

It must have appeared to old ladies who combed their Bibles at New England firesides that the days of Pharaoh had come again and the whole list of plagues was once more to descend upon the wretched land for its unnatural sin. The Bible was called in, and from its Sybilline pages it was shewn by one side that slavery was wrong, by the other that it was right; and the basis of the American political fabric was discussed with opposite and contradictory results. The struggle of words and reasons continued as the prelude to the struggle of force.

It was argued that slavery was immoral, that it caused licentious intercourse between the races and destroyed virtue among the Negro females, that it broke up families and was otherwise very cruel. To this it was replied that the slaves had by nature no chastity to lose, that their condition was far happier than that of the free laborer at the North, it being to the interest of the master to feed, clothe, and protect his slaves.

All these discussions awoke the ingenuity of the Southern mind, not heretofore much given to such themes. And here it is curious to note what acute reasons can be found for even a bad thing, said thing being in some respects judged valuable. It was argued here at the South that the Negro was not fit and never could be a free man, that God had deliberately made him deficient. That it would be an inhuman deed to free him as he would surely perish. That, after all, slavery checked the spread of agrarianism and hence was beneficial to all sections of the Union. Finally, some bold speculator, by a favor granted to him alone, entered the secret councils of Heaven and learned that the Creator never intended that the Negro should improve mentally and morally! That, in short, the Abolitionists knew nothing of the matter and had best "let us alone" which, if they cared for the Union and the Constitution, they were bound to do.

The agitation grew apace, but reached no solution. Gold entered too largely into this problem to allow the argument or the literature which grew up about this subject to have for its object anything like the finding of the truth. Outside foes are sometimes the safeguards of nations. Had there been at this time west of the Mississippi a strong and watchful enemy the several states would have grown more closely together and found cause to value their Union, but formidable foe there was none, and the Western regions were soon to become the occasion of combat between the sections. Toward the West the South looked with eager eyes: the rich acres lured its peculiar tendencies. There a great slave empire was to arise. A new source of wealth offered itself to the settlers. Every man was to be a greater slave owner than before; and, with the extension of slavery westward, the South would gain power to control the Government and thus protect that slave interest against which such strenuous opposition had arisen.

Gold, the great national god, had spoken; the ear of the devout people heard no other sound. Zeus himself had never thundered so loud. The glitter of the divinity blinded the eyes of most. Justice had taken wing, now afar invisible in the clouds, and Truth—at all times hard to see—now vanished from sight completely. The time for thinking had not yet come to America. Art, science, the quiet culture of the individual, all that mental and moral wealth which were beginning to characterize the older nations of Europe had not yet received their due value here. Material good was the goal of the people.

The South saw its growing inferiority with deep discontent. One by one the Southern dreams vanished as the vast new territories became the spoil of the free soil party. The tracts between the Mississippi and Ohio Rivers became theirs. A geographical line was unwillingly agreed upon as the limit beyond which the foot of slavery should not trespass. The West too was to exclude the Southern man if he owned slaves. The gold of California was not to be dug by him; and now, after having fought through the Mexican War, Texas, a vast empire in itself, was to have its gates shut against the slave owner. Therefore he felt that his equality under the Constitution was practically denied. The laws had become rotten wishes. If his slaves escaped, they were to be free. They were encouraged to escape. They were not property and should not exist as such beyond certain limits, and all this in defiance of the fugitive slave laws. In all this the South saw the edict of final emancipation and felt that slavery, if it did not advance, at no distant day must perish and with it the then basis of Southern wealth.

In 1850 the Southern delegates of convention met at Nashville to concert means of protection and redress. They aimed to defend themselves under the shield of the Constitution. They read that instrument according to the spirit and sentiment of the times when it was devised. They well knew how fanatical the love of self government at that time was, with what jealous distrust power had been entrusted to a General Government, how great was then the fear of centralization, and the ideas of that time they applied to the issues of their own day. The new wine they intended to put into the old wineskins.

They found what they most wanted to find, that the Constitution was a "compact" between independent state governments and that the several states were the creators of the General Government, that the object of this compact had failed and that Secession was legal and in conformity with the whole history and nature of the

American system. At the North, on the other hand, the idea of the Government had greatly modified itself. In the minds of the people the Federal Union had become a national republic. For them the Government had only blessings. They were not trammeled by any institution like that of slavery which they must jealously defend against the other states and against the world. Among them it resulted that the idea of disunion was utterly intolerable. It would not be; it could not be; finally, it must not be!

Could the claims of state sovereignty be carried out? Could Secession be peaceable? Or, would not both parties "camp outside" of the Constitution. The statesmen of the time saw with sane clearness that the country, constantly growing at it was, was in fact outgrowing the Constitution. The Union which was first called a league of states was next called a Government "of the people," and finally developed itself into a nation. It was clear also to many who were not entirely blinded by self interest that this natural progress of things each year added to the impossibility of "peaceable Secession."

Here let us pause awhile and view this mighty scene of natural progress, self interest, and passion: let us climb above the lower mists, mount some mental height above the fogs of prejudice, and look down upon the scene. What do we behold? Men of honest aims and following long inherited opinions struggling to uphold slavery against the entire world, barbarism against civilization, the Middle Ages against modern life! A tremendous effort! The forces against them they miscalculated. To succeed they must do no less than bind the stronger North and West by the outgrown ideas of a fast changing political system.

Vast territories had been acquired to the Government by the Louisiana Purchase and the War with Mexico of 1846, and new free states formed out of these, created by the Government, greater in extent than the entire area of the thirteen original colonies on the Atlantic Coast. These new states as the creations and not the creators of the Government naturally took their stand on the part of the central power. White population poured into the New World and moved westward; and, spurred by its needs and energy, the wealth, the commerce, and industries of the North and West grew into great proportions. The power and importance of the

Union grew in the minds of all. No longer the mere offspring of "the people" or of "sovereign independent states" as it originally was, the General Government assumed a well defined position and reality. Sprung of the same race, of the same general position in life, enjoying the same degree of freedom, and having the same aims and methods, it was possible for the people of the North and West to form a solid and homogeneous Society, a Society which was in a normal condition. Against these odds the Southern section, with its "peculiar institution," with its abnormal Society, had to maintain its existence, nay, had to keep itself dominant.

Through the skill and genius of its leaders, the slave section succeeded in making prominent for a long time the doctrine of state sovereignty and, by implication, the right of the states to secede from the Union—or "compact" in the language of the time. They succeeded in long maintaining slave property as a legal right and one upheld by the Constitution; and, through their insistence and the willingness of the Northern people to compromise matters, the fugitive slave laws were carried out by which the legal right of owners over escaped slaves was enforced in the very citadels of abolition itself.

As a proof of the long continued success of the South in this political contest, the following facts are worthy of note. In the period from 1789 to 1861 there were eleven Southern Presidents out of a total of sixteen; judges of Supreme Court, seventeen Southern out of twenty-eight; Attorneys General of U.S., fourteen out of nineteen; Presidents of the Senate, sixty-one out of seventy-seven; Speakers of the House, twenty-one out of thirty-three. These results of public contest indicate the struggle of the South for power and the vital interest felt by that section in politics.

The election of Lincoln in 1861 [sic] by the Republican Party acted as the touchstone of antagonistic sections. The times were ripe; the issue was at hand. The cloak fell from the face of the Truth, and what was revealed? That the Union which had long ceased to exist in thought now existed no longer in fact. The Constitution, the revered, the perpetual of the Fathers, faded away. On the one side stood the great nation of the North and West; on the other in the position of antagonists stood with one accord the slave states of the South. The sections crystallized together as water when reaching the freezing point suddenly passes into compact ice. The Union of free and sovereign states was at an end. The rule of Force took the place of the rule of Reason. War governments were established on both sides. The American system of polity had met a first and decisive disaster.

It is not our aim to enter into the details of the war which followed. Its result was that the seceding states which were supposed to have been sovereign and to have been the early creators of the Government were by that Government subdued, reduced to the condition of conquered provinces, and finally allowed after some years of repentance to become organized again as states subject to the General Government. The conquerors wisely determined to remove the cause of any future antagonism, to destroy the seeds of future revolt. Believing the cause to reside in the existence of slavery and the rule of oligarchies, the domination of the many by the irresponsible rule of the few, they abolished slavery from the South and afterwards conferred upon the slaves the power of the ballot without qualification. Thus at last! after the fierce antagonisms of one hundred years, the unrest, the hatred, the vituperation, and after a cruel appeal to blood and iron, the South and North were at length one—one in their Social systems, one in the equal rights of manhood. Arms should be hung upon their walls, and a Pax Americana spread its quiet wings over the land!

The victors really thought that all these results were accomplished. They hoped for the best, and many of the vanquished valued at its true worth the earnestness of these convictions. The conquerors acted on the belief that a slave race of untold centuries could be and were made freemen and citizens, not by the slow process of race growth, but by a decree of Government. That these freemen could be and were made citizens, not by their mental and moral elevation among their fellows, but by giving them civil and political rights which they had not made for themselves. The attempt was made in good faith to confer upon the slave that political freedom which the white race itself had been engaged for some fifty generations, with a very varying success, in creating and building up. The attempt has not been a success. The conditions of success were not present. The experiment was a highly unnatural one. After twenty-five years of uncertainty and confusion a state of equilibrium seems to have established itself.

If heavy boulders of rock be thrown into the bed of a stream as it moves toward the sea, its waters for the instant pause, they foam and whirl and change their course; it appears to the looker on that the stream has been checked; but, on going further down its banks, its waters are found once again quietly pursuing their way, their speed still determined as it was before, meeting the obstruction by its volume of water and the slope of its bed. Its natural conditions, temporarily disturbed, have reasserted themselves.

Very much the same thing has happened at the South. Freedom has been suddenly given the Negro for the first time in the history of his race. The "right" of the ballot, one of the last fruits of civilization, has been conferred upon him. He has not manifested an ability to use or to perpetuate these acquired "rights." He has not asserted strenuously or intelligently his equal right to rule along with the white, nor has he made any real attempt to dominate them, however in the majority. The whites also have assumed pretty much their old position. They control all the Southern states, be they in the minority or not. The few still rule the many. This is the old condition of equilibrium at the South; and the old political antagonism remains and quickly springs up against any party or measure that threatens to disturb this equilibrium. In short, many of these causes which all through its history kept the South in a state of antagonism to the rest of the Union were not removed by the war because force, however skillfully applied, could not remove them without expelling one of the two races. They were not removed by legal enactment because no laws of human device can build over a Society in a limited period of time.

There are moral impossibilities in nature just as there are physical impossibilities in nature. There is no scheme by which a quart of water can be got into a pint cup—nor steam generated by the application of cold. Nor is there any law by which the slave can be changed into the free citizen, except by the law of the gradual process of human development under better conditions and under changed conditions.

In the first part of this chapter we have been endeavouring to point the effects which African slavery has produced in the states. We have seen the effects upon the minds and methods of the white race and the slave-owning class: how it influenced the state governments and originated a political system antagonistic to the policy of the free states. That as a final result it has prevented the affiliation of the South with the North and West and [has] been the source of a terrific civil war; and, that since that time the presence of the same race, diverse in birth, in character and morals, has been a source of unrest and tended still to keep alive the feeling of antagonism of the old slave states against the General Government, an effect which still continues.

We will now look at the other side of the picture and see what has been the effect produced upon the African by his enforced residence among the whites of America. There is sometimes "a spirit of goodness in things evil." It is strange indeed that force, armed force, has indirectly done so much toward moving on the civilization of the world. How often has it been that a conquering nation has spread its best victories, not by teaching, but by arms: how often has the vanquished been the greater gainer by receiving from his conqueror what he never aimed to give—his arts, his sciences, and his laws. These are the things of history that make one think, where results are so very different from the aims sought by the actors in the scene.

This is markedly true of the Negro in this country, brought here by force and by force kept in bondage. He has received and is now receiving what was never intended to be given by his masters. He, the slave, has moved more rapidly forward from his position of African savagery, forced by a higher civilization, inoculated with the leaven of the white race, than the white race itself has moved forward from its own past condition, forced by no higher civilization. Until now in 1895, as one looks curiously backward over two hundred and forty years of African slavery, the fact grows clear that the race, despite the period of seemingly dead bondage, despite the opposition of its rulers, obeying a natural law of progress, has received of the whites some of the best treasures they had to give, and of recent years has received them almost free. So far as they can take and make them theirs, whether intelligently or by imitation, two thousand years of civilization have been and are being slowly injected into the Africans whether they seek it or not, by a surrounding time spirit from which they cannot escape.

In its effect upon the Negro, slavery was not a system of mere degradation. It was a sort of government and school of training. This was a necessity of the case; and, altho' it is true that this training school had for its aim not the Negro's but the white man's benefit, it was impossible for him to escape from some influence for good which it exercised. The necessity of daily toil was in itself a great educator; for, although the usual work in Southern fields was very simple, still it could not be done without some degree of intelligence and care. These qualities the Negro did not naturally possess; he had to acquire them under the supervision of the whites. The slave, in order that he become valuable, had to abandon the customs and habits of Africa and become more of a human being.

The hand-to-mouth life of his native land, the subsistence on fruits, roots, bark of trees and vermin, the indulgence in the eating of human flesh, all these means of precarious livelihood and the slothful habits thereto belonging, he was driven to relinquish as soon as he came within range of the white man's power. Nor was the master's power from one standpoint as irresponsible as one may imagine. It was controlled by many considerations. These were mainly considerations of self interest. The slave was very dear to the owner. The life of the slave was of primary consequence because in addition to the value of his work he represented a money value in his own person. His well-being in a physical sense was therefore more guarded than that of any class of free labor is at present.

The overseers and "drivers," the latter usually of their own race, were by no means the monsters often described. Against them the slave could always appeal to the master and commonly did so. The use of this liberty on the part of the Negroes often brought about some very complicated results. In case of disputes between overseer and slave, the master often found himself irresistibly led to take the slave's part: the slave thus came to look down on the working white man, overseer or other, and up to his owner who grew to be in his eyes a superior being immensely removed above the common fate of humanity. The slaves looked upon themselves as necessary to their owners and bound up with their interest, and they expected and received a great degree of kindness and leniency. A mutual bond was thus established between the very low and the very high which was not easily destroyed and which exists with pathetic reality to the present day, although thirty years have since elapsed, despite the violent changes due to war and despite the incitements to distrust and ill will which have since arisen. Southerners of the old regime are still the advisers, the benefactors, and to some extent the supporters of multitudes of Negroes whose parents they inherited from their fathers, who lived on their lands, worked some four or five hours a day, and never felt the weight of a lash during the course of their lives; and one frequently hears the old words "boss" and "massa" coming from their lips with a strange fidelity to the old relations.

The Southern plantation was a little Society within itself. It had its work proportioned to the age and sex of its members and adjusted also to the strength or weakness of the workers. It had its various trades also. The carpenters, the bricklayers, the smiths, the boatmen, the ginners of cotton and the threshers of rice, all had well defined duties. In fine, much of that knowledge of farming and the mechanic arts by which they have been able since their freedom to earn their bread they derived from their taskmasters of the old days. The plantations had also their system of laws, of punishments, and rewards. The majority of these looked to the well-being of the slaves directly. They were aimed against lazyness, against domestic immorality and the habit of stealing which was common. Strangely enough, these laws were often put in force and the punishments for disobedience meted out by Negroes and not by whites. Negro foremen inspected the day's work, and Negro foremen also administered punishment for infraction of the rules and laws of the plantation. In this way they were in a certain sense their own directors and rulers.

A kind of police system or "patrol" was kept up in some parts of the country. The object of this provision has been so entirely misunderstood by many who know nothing of the South, of slavery, that some remark on it may not be out of place here.[1] The patrol

[1] And, perhaps some "remark" on Seabrook's interpretation of the patrol law is necessary. As pointed out in the introduction, it is all too obvious that regulations of this sort were designed to maintain strict order and to suppress slave revolts.

system was not intended to prevent the insurrection of Negroes against the whites. Of the danger of such a thing the whites seldom thought. But the real aim of the patrol was to keep the Negroes at home and prevent the slaves of one farm or plantation [from] committing thefts and depredations upon an adjoining one. When depredations of this sort occurred or a fight took place between slaves of different owners, the masters were brought into collision with each other, and especially was this the case if a slave detected in the act of theft was punished by some person to whom he did not belong. As to the danger of slave insurrection and the deep-seated hatred to the whites which may naturally be supposed to have burned in their breasts, one may judge the reality of all this when we remember that during the Civil War, when the white men were often absent and their women and children were left unguarded behind them and at the mercy of these very people, Negro insurrections were unknown and unprotected women slept in profound safety though surrounded by Negroes and living at great distances from each other.

Proper rearing of the young and care of the sick and the infirm were also enjoined upon them, and habits of domestic virtue were also encouraged, as far as was possible among a people who naturally were not impressed with the value of marital fidelity or chastity. They were also taught many things which were directly useful to the whites and to themselves in the system under which both lived. One of these was the use of figures, the habit of calculation, but they were not allowed to read or write for such knowledge would be inimical to the system of a peaceful contented subjection. It would never do that the Negroes should be allowed to read "abolition" tracts and to sit up o'nights spelling out "abolition" doctrines over the glare of blazing pine knots in their dingy little cabins. If they did so, those cabins might begin to look too small, and the morrow's ill-paid work might come to look discouraging. For a like reason, Negro preachers were discountenanced, and white clergymen were called in by the masters to conduct religious services among them.

But the best influence to which the slaves were subjected was the presence of the slave owners themselves. These people formed the most refined class at the South. They had ample leisure for culture. They were most of them men and women of the world and were controlled by liberal ideas. They were not governed in their conduct toward their slaves by greed, nor did they generally exercise toward them the harder virtues which the man of business and the man of affairs lay down as rules for others to live by.[2] And besides all this, they knew the Negro well. They saw wherein lay his strength and his weakness, his virtues and his vices. Their rule was usually lenient and as just as possible in a system where justice was not a characteristic. The class of masters stood as the mediator between the slave and the natural harshness and injustice of the system itself. The interests of the two tended to become more and more identified with each other. The institution of slavery from generation to generation by the same family of whites, the traditions of the past, the remembrance of bygone faithful service—all interwove the personal sympathies of the master and the slave. The relation among the better class of owners lost much of its character of subjection by force and became a domestic institution. The welfare of the slave grew to be a matter of personal feeling with the owner, and the owner in the mind of the slave acquired a divine right of control. Rule of the slave by the lash gave way to rule by moral influence. Slavery was, in its worst features, tending to disappear, and with process of time freedom was becoming more and more possible. Both the gradual improvement in the habits of the slaves themselves and industrial and commercial changes in the country would ultimately have made the costly system of slave labor an impossibility. If for no other reason, it would have ceased to pay, and the large sums of money therein invested been better employed otherwise.

One sees it often stated, and with an air of some triumph, what great advances the Negroes have made since their emancipation. This view of the matter is superficial and comes of ignorance of the past condition of that race. Let us rather say that it is only since his freedom that the Negro is in a position to exhibit before the world those better traits and abilities which his race had developed during the long tutelage of slavery. A better man, a

[2] Again Seabrook paints a much too optimistic picture of the Old South. The writings of Frederick Law Olmstead on the eve of the Civil War hardly substantiate this portrait of a cultured, liberal, refined master class. Even if one grants Seabrook's assumptions, personal contact between owner and slave was extremely limited—hence this "cultured" influence upon the mass of Negroes was virtually nil.

wiser man than the brute African had been growing within him, but this "new man" remained concealed within his bosom, hid in the depths of his consciousness, peering out at times patiently for the signs of a better day, but not yet conscious enough, not yet strong enough to assert his existence and make or demand a better destiny.

The Southern people who believe that they knew the Negro best were themselves deceived as to the kind and amount of progress which that people had made. The long training had worked better than the trainers suspected. Thus it was that freedom, although so suddenly conferred, found them in some sense prepared for the change. The actual transformation of life was by no means so violent as a fanciful view may lead one to think.

The habit of earning a living the slave race had long acquired. After the Civil War their way of life lay plain before them. The industries of the South had not materially changed and with those kinds of occupation they were well acquainted. The whites of the South were compelled to engage still their services in all the industries of the country and most of those of the cities. The Negroes moreover had this great point in their favor: they were not subjected to the competition of any other working class. Nor indeed was it easy then, nor is it so now, to find any class of workers more fitted to the simple field occupation of that section than the race which has so long been engaged therein.

But with the benefits heretofore mentioned the educational value of slavery ceased. If it tended to improve the Negro race in a moral and material way, in the matter of better habits and organized work, it cannot be maintained that it tended to make the serf a citizen. The moral qualities which a life of subjection instilled into its subjects were not those which make an independent and self-reliant citizen. Under slavery the Negroes never developed any ambition, nor respect for themselves as a race, nor as individuals. In fact, this feeling of individuality, of self assertion is the very quality which under slavery they could not acquire. And yet, these are the qualities which as citizens they must exercise. That they have not done so, that they have shewn little power in the claiming or exercise of their public rights is the result which must logically be expected as brought about by the past influences of their lives.

2

Race Conflicts

A spirit of kinship shews itself everywhere. The otherwise loose and erratic elements of nature are bound together into unity and self perpetuation. The atoms of minerals cohere and form crystals of definite shape; chemical bodies seek each other with energy and continue according to fixed laws. These phenomena are something more than mere facts; they exhibit an active power of attraction, a sort of self determination. For want of a better name we call this power affinity, not knowing what it is. In the world of life the same feeling of kinship prevails, and its exhibitions are equally marked. Plants and animals range themselves into groups and families with a persistence marvelous and regular.

The races of men, be they civilized or not, exhibit the same law. The members of the same race have for each other a strong active coherence, a natural sympathy, and toward a different race an absence of such sympathy. More than any other influence this tendency has ruled the history of men. The races of the world have kept themselves more or less distinct. They who looked upon themselves as the superior have gone even so far as to deny to the inferior the right to be classed as men at all and [have] acted in accordance with this feeling. This coherence of a race with itself and lack of sympathy with a different race is the great fact which has always rendered slavery possible. The enslaver feels that he does no wrong when he holds in subjection the alien and the

64

stranger; but, when he enslaves members of his own race, presently the sense of race sympathy asserts itself and the moral aspect of the question begins to awake in his mind.

Therefore, we find that in obedience to this feeling at a very early day the question arose as to whether a Greek had a right to enslave a Greek; and, if he did so, what special privileges ought to be given the person so held, but the question did not arise as to whether he had the right to enslave other races. The subjection of aliens was regarded as proper; in their case no question of right or wrong could arise. They were aliens and that was enough. In a modified form, the same truth confronts us today all over this land. Slavery is absent; but the black race and the white race are distinct. The white man sympathizes with his race; the black man, with his. The affinity of each with itself is greater under all circumstances than the affinity of either with the other. And, it is very important to note that this sympathy is ever active and rules the conduct of each race whether they will it or no.

We may delude ourselves with ever so much belief in our humanity and our philanthropy, but charity to the whites is a far stronger motive with us than charity to the blacks; justice to the whites makes a stronger demand upon us than justice to the blacks. The poverty of the whites may be a matter of some solicitude, but the penury of the blacks is taken as a matter of course. The Negroes on their part are moved by the same feelings. Living in the presence of the white race, their first care is for their own people; and, if their unity is not so complete, it is only because their passions are not so keen and because they distrust each other.

Thus, coherence between the two races at the South is weak and easily disturbed. In this absence of an active sympathy neither race is animated with a desire to benefit the other; neither feels a necessity to respect the other's rights. There may not be active conflict, but there is indifference; and, where the rights of the one clash with the rights of the other, where the advantage of the one is opposed to the advantage of the other, the feeling of indifference quickly passes into the feeling of antagonism. If the two peoples were not bound together in the same geographical limits in this country and if their separation would not entail on each immediate disasters which both recognize, it is certain that the two races would abandon each other, each going his own way as naturally as oil and water when poured into the same vessel seek different levels.

The lack of racial sympathy shews itself in the relentless claim of superiority which one of the races sets up: a claim which has all along been made and which is still in full force. The status of ruler and ruled is constantly cropping out. Not only in taking slaves from the coast of Africa without their consent, but afterwards when in order to introduce reform and repress the slave trade England placed warships upon their coast—contrary to the expressed wish of the African kings themselves—has the assertion of superiority been evident. This condition of things under one or another name still goes on. The whites still assert and assume the right of control over the blacks on the same grounds.

Whether as servant and master, as workman and "boss," in matters of church government, in elections, the same thing appears. We are always the chosen people and have a divine patent of nobility! The copper colored, the yellow, and the black races are always the heathen and the gentiles. "The Lord has delivered them into our hand." "We will lead their sons and daughters captive." What a comfortable doctrine is this! how antique and reverend with age! How consoling it must have been to the conqueror when he consulted his priests and augurs to be told that not his own selfish greed, but the voice of his god enjoined upon him the plunder and subjection of aliens! We have still our priests and augurs who interpret for us our wishes and unfortunately there are still to be found the Canaanites, the Hittites, and the Perisites [sic].

Before the war of liberation, the Negro secretly chafed under the system of unpaid labor, a system whose chief hardship, as we see it now, consisted not so much in the amount of toil or the actual cruelty of today, as in denying to its victims all hope of tomorrow, all chance of betterment. It was a method of mental and moral inaction. On this depended its success. And, since the war of liberation, they who aimed, made laws, and finally fought to maintain this state of things now blame and contemn those, their victims, because they have neither minds nor morals. "See how unthinking you are; how slothful in habit; how unchaste in life; how ignorant of the values of truth and the cost of falsehood; how full of secrecy. You are an inferior race; stay where you are and keep to yourselves as much as possible." So says the white man at the South, in fact, the white race all over the country. And thus act the nations of Europe in the several "spheres of their influence" in Africa at the present moment.

And, what is the reply of the other race? A kind of dumb acquiescense. A wonder as to what the white man means by his vigorous assertions: an indifference to his claims, coupled with a readiness to return next day into the company of the whites without manifesting any remembrance of such treatment and at times even exhibiting their innate love for the show of power by attaching "Captain" or "Major" to the white men's names. Such is the other side of the "Race Conflict" so-called. Is it not possible to doubt its reality? Are the conditions for a real conflict present? Or, is it not the rather probable that the active aggression is on the part of the whites?

The following is a homely illustration, but one that makes food for reflection. On going through the streets of a Southern town one may often see the following occurrence. Two children are playing together. One is white and dirty; the other black and dirtier. It is so common that no one notices it. The white child proposes that they shall "play horse." The miniature cart is hauled out from its shed, and the white child quietly seats himself therein, and the black horse takes up the shaft to pull. Presently the "horse" gets tired or would like to be pulled in his turn. This the other fails to understand and probably walks off, both deaf and blind. These children are "playing horse" now; presently they will be engaged in working and ruling on the same plan. This is a sample of the race conflict in its egg.

The rather unreal nature of the race conflict, as far as the Negroes are party to it, appears very strikingly in the following considerations. There is no opposition shewn toward him by the whites in matters of business. He is free to trade by wholesale or retail, to go into any market, to offer goods to any buyer, as cheap or cheaper than the whites, to bank his money and to invest as he chooses, free to start any enterprise, to erect mills, to establish printing presses and issue his literature devoted to his own ends and needs. If he were stirred by a keen sense of hostility, it would naturally find expression in the use of money and in the conduct of these varied practical affairs which consume so large a part of the energy of everyday life. Negro trades and Negro stores, Negro banks and papers would easily come into being, concern themselves entirely with the interests of that race, and hold tenaceously [sic] a position of opposition to the similar institutions of the whites.

But, such is not the case, nor does anyone hear ever a suggestion of the kind distinctly stated. The idea of competition seems not to enter their minds. They live from the white men's stores, work for their companies, adopt their latest fashions of dress, and—when they read—read their papers. In all these respects, to use their formulated expression, "The white people let the 'niggers' alone," and a degree of easy-going harmony prevails. And the question naturally arises, if they were or could be equally "let alone" in certain other matters by the Democratic and Republican parties, whether the same results would not follow. But this seems to be impossible, at least at present, for one party excites their hostility with more or less success against the Southern whites; the other party excites their fears and suspicions by shewing a constant disposition to deprive them of their rights. Thus, in either way, do the whites demand the subserviency of the Negro and make him subject to their ends. Thus is the theory of his equality practically denied by both his friends and foes. This contradictory state of things is so suggestive that it merits further treatment which we will reserve for a future page.

As a matter of daily experience it is seldom one hears a wish expressed [by Negroes] to go where they are not asked, either in private houses or churches, vehicles, sitting rooms at depots, restaurants, or any place whatsoever set apart by the whites for their own use. Or, if for any purpose they are called into parlors or business offices, they will usually stand until asked to be seated and will even then usually select some unobtrusive bench or chair on which to locate themselves. One who has lived at the South and been brought by the work of daily life into close personal contact with that race, especially if he comes of the class of slave owners and therefore retains a sense of good will toward them and a perception of their anomalous present position in life, is generally tempted to smile when he is told about "an ineradicable race conflict" on their part and is not easily alarmed by the bugaboo of politicians wishing to keep office and willing to make both whites and blacks legitimate prey, the former through the medium of their fears, the latter through the medium of their ignorance and docility.

But the slave-holding class, with their tolerance for the Negroes and their wise and moderate habits of personal control, is now almost extinct. The mantle of their good will they have not left behind them to the men of the "New South." Between the Southerner of the old regime and the Negro no cause of conflict can or does easily arise; it seems unnatural to both. But the man of the "New South," the active working man of affairs, from whatever section he comes, feels quite differently. For him the Negro is worthy of regard because he can be used; beyond this he has no value or interest, and there the matter ends. He has no sympathy for the race and no cause of personal attachment to the individual.

It is very likely that in those feelings which bind together man and man the two races are now much further apart than they were twenty years ago. The days are well nigh past when Southern parents teach their children the duty of personal respect toward family servants or encourage them to visit their homes and minister to their wants. "Our white people," once a favorite phrase among the Negroes, is more seldom heard than it once was; the relation having passed away with the life of the old generation.

A line of separation clearly seen by both races has taken its place. On the one side stands the white race, not of the South only, but of the whole country, a unit in sentiment and actively aggressive, seeking their own advantage in all things whether of private business or politics. On the other side are the blacks, neither progressive nor aggressive, full of mutual distrust and devoid of stable unity, their chief means of defence being their adaptation to the climate and occupations of the section where they are most collected. In the meantime there are changes going on. The industries of the South are no longer purely agricultural. Enterprises are increasing in number and variety. New means of employment are opening up and giving occupation to an increased number of white workmen. The question of work and wages must inevitably keep stimulating the whites against the blacks. Even now the employer who shews a preference for Negro labor or uses toward them some degree of tolerance and leniency is apt to excite ill will and abuse. In the minds of the white workman such an employer is a protector and friend of "niggers" and hence an enemy of his own race.

But, this feeling is not new. The slavocrat with his black retinue was always an object of dislike to the white working class at the South. He represented the degradation of labor: the hated principle of work without fair pay. Instinctively the sense of self-preservation makes free labor the natural foe of the slave and the slave owner wherever the two exist together on a large or on a small scale. There was an abolition party and a little war against slavery going on in every one of the Southern states and based on the same causes which afterwards armed section against section and ended in the Civil War. These local feuds did not have their origin in sentiment, philanthropy, or any desire for justice toward the slaves; but, they arose from the fact that the white farmers and mechanical work-men of the South perceived that the low wages which the slaves got in the form of shelter, food, and clothes rendered all competition with them impossible, practically drove away the white laborer and annulled his chances of life.

The industrial white population of the South has the same feeling still. The contest between white labor and black labor, which is by far the most serious aspect of the race question, has its roots in a very simple fact. The Negro's needs are few; his demands upon life are small. A simple house, often a mere hut, simple food, and com-mon clothing are usually the sum of his wants. The more costly habits, the many fancies, passions, vanities, and ambitions of the white race—all of which cost money—do not belong to the Negro. His life in general costs him less; therefore, in the competition for wages, he is able without hardship and without sense of suffering to underbid easily the superior race: this the white man knows. His pay and the value of his work, whatever he may think of its superior merit, he sees to be modified by the pay of the other race; or, at least that there is a strong tendency on the part of em-ployers so to modify it.

Take the following example. A mill is in process of building. A body of skilled mechanics is engaged to erect it, locate the machinery, test its working, and put it in operation. They are paid in proportion to the value of their special work for the time being. Then it often happens that their work and pay are both at an end. Gradually one by one they are dismissed for economic reasons, and the cheaper labor of the blacks is called in to find steady employment and reap the fruit of the work that other men's hands have constructed. It is true that these men have not been driven away; but, if they remain, they must reduce their expectation of pay to the price at which the Negroes will probably work. And, if they do this, they practically destroy their own basis of work and accept pay on which they cannot live and support their families, while the Negro with his simple wants manages to live and support his. The perception of this fact does not make the white man who has his living to get the friend of the black.

Workmen who are native to the South are somewhat inured to this state of things; but, workmen who chance to come into the South look about them, then begin to doubt, and finally come out openly and express their sense of outrage and disgust at the status of work and the kind of competition to which they are subjected. For them, bred perhaps in an atmosphere of work which is both respectable and well paid, the South with its coarser labor and poor pay, with its workmen of a race which does not respect itself and is not respected, is merely a "nigger country."

Southerners of the employer class who countenance and hire Negroes, permit them to live on their premises at easy rates, and in some sort protect and assist them, are looked upon as "friends of the 'coons,' " and the contemptuous remark is added, "They suit each other very well! Let them stay together. The South is no good!" So says the emigrant workman. What does he mean by these remarks? Simply this. The Negro competition to which he finds himself subjected is against his interest. It greatly reduces his chance of employment; or, if he is employed, reduces his rate of wages. Naturally he must accept the terms he finds, and he is in some measure angry against the white race of the South because, in his view of the matter, they encourage the Negro and discourage the whites. There is in the bottom of his mind the feeling that it is the duty of Southern employers to find work for their own race, despite other considerations and to get rid of the Negroes as far as may be [possible].

It is thought by many that the emigrant does not come to the South because he is not well treated, because the Southerner has a natural preference for the Negro and does not respect the dignity of labor. So long, it is said, have the Southern people been used to the degraded nature of work that they still persist in applying the same ideas and shewing the same feelings toward all workmen in general, whatever their worth or capacity. And then, "They don't treat the emigrant right."

This explanation is only partially true. The more radical explanation is this. The white workman, be he native or emigrant, in the matter of wages has to meet the Negro population and compete with them very often on their own ground. The living wages of the Negro are lower than those of the whites. The one demands high pay and demands many things for his comfort which he regards as necessities. These he must have or his work bears no fruit. The other race demands comparatively little. Those things which to the whites are necessities are often to the Negro useless superfluities. He is able therefore to work cheaper and does so. The white workman of the South suffers in the same way that the emigrant does. In the matter of bread winning they are both in sympathy with each other.

So then, the labor problem at the South is complicated by the presence of the two races. These races are so unlike that they do not permit of a homogeneous basis of work or wages. The employer is forced to adopt annoying distinctions of all sorts, and his mind becomes full of all kinds of inventions by which he may do justice to both classes of employees without alienating either.

Where the people stand contrasted in the character of their work and further contrasted in the amount of their pay, where each race feels differently toward the employer, and where that employer acts in different ways toward each of them, where there are no "labor unions" for self-protection against greed of capital, but rather "race unions" which represent the competition of race with race, it will be readily seen that out of this basis of discord and unfriendship in the primary matter of bread winning there can scarsely arise any unanimity of interest in public affairs.

The unhappy complications pointed out are the outcome of differences in race. They have not been produced by the war. The emancipation of the Negro has not created them—nor are they willfully concocted by the natural deviltry of either race therein concerned. The fact is that the races, particularly the Negroes, are rather disposed toward peaceable relations so far as possible and under the difficulties of the case succeed wonderfully well. "Race conflict" [and] "race war" are not the proper words to use to describe the relations accurately: we should rather say race contrast. The remedy for the industrial troubles of which we are speaking consists not in pulling the white man down by discouraging skilled labor, but by pulling the Negro up. In the matter of employment he must become an intelligent and painstaking workman who shall respect himself and his occupation. This can only be done by the spread of education and the improvement of the life and habits of the Negro. Time and the growth of time alone can work it out; and, when finally the work of both races, having more equalized value, shall have become fixed on the same basis of pay, a union of labor at the South may be possible. Labor unions will not then be race unions; and, the healthy relation of labor and capital, no longer complicated with race questions, become[s] the normal state of things.

In religious matters the segregation of the races seems to be very complete. Contest between them on purely religious grounds does not occur. The creed, ideas, or religious usages of the Negro do not conflict with the other race. However strongly the religious sentiments of the two may be contrasted, there is no active motive for antagonism. So great is the diversity of modern creeds and so transcendental are the subjects of interest that the men of the modern world are pretty well agreed to let each person have his own heaven as his reason or his fancy may dictate and to let him journey thither by his own road or by no road at all. In this matter all men's intentions are supposed to be good.

And besides, we of the United States are a very practical people. Our eyes are directed toward this vast and young continent which we are engaged in peopling, cultivating, and wresting from the domain of wild nature. That which is above us we do not see. That which is spiritual we have no time to search out. Our time is enclosed in the limits of today; our interest is in what the day may bring forth. No set of people, even if not divided by the most glaring differences of race, is much concerned in what the others may think or do as to the salvation of their immortal souls. The question would rather be as to whether a large part of our very practical multitude believe that they have any souls in the first instance; or, if they do, whether the universal "all rightness" of American life is not in itself heaven enough without looking for anything beyond. It is to be feared that such is the case.

Christianity has within it a spirit which seizes upon the consciousness of all peoples and races. The savage man and the cultured, the fool and the thinker all hear in it a voice which speaks to each and feel a power which flows into every man according to his ability to receive. The Negro race has fallen under its spell. They have received its spirit and accepted its teachings so far as their mental and moral structure and the still active remembrance of African superstitions have permitted them to do—strangely and weirdly and dimly very often, but still with some degree of success. This growth of the Negroes in religious instruction is regarded by all people at the South with satisfaction. For, whatever a man may think or feel about religious matters for himself, he usually prefers to see others with whom he has to do influenced by religious motives and, in some sense, be it only in a rude way, subject to its [sic] restraints.

But here candor compels one to say the complaisance of the Southern white ends. So long as the Negroes keep within the limits of their own religious organizations, it is well; but, if or whenever the Negroes wish to influence the like organizations of the whites by representations in their church government and in their conventions, then the whites assume the role of the opposition and the distinction of race is insisted on.[1] Nothing better exhibits the temper of the South in this matter of the exercise of power than the fact that even in matters of religion where all men are supposed to stand on the same ground and where there is theoretically no distinction of persons, one of the races insists on maintaining those natural distinctions which divide man from man and race from

[1] As noted in the introduction, in 1887 Seabrook's father fought for the seating of Negro churchmen at the state convention of the Episcopal Church of South Carolina. Prevented from delivering a full statement, he later published an extensive pamphlet containing his views.

race. The claims of race assert themselves superior to the claims of creed. Pride, power, wealth, and the strong influences of past history demand superior recognition here as in the other relations of life.

It is true that in the Northern states these distinctions do not exist with such vitality, but there the conditions are essentially different from what they are at the South. A small minority of Negroes is lost in the overwhelming white population there and can in no very marked way make itself felt. But, if the black, rough-hewn multitude of Mississippi or South Carolina were moved into the state of Massachusetts, it is interesting to surmise what effects would follow. We will not attempt an answer to this supposition but content ourselves by saying that since all people are controlled by much the same feelings, it is likely that many of the same results would come about which have developed themselves here, with the difference that as the two peoples would be unaccustomed to each other the immediate contact would be less harmonious than at the South.

The struggle for influence in the government and the administration of law is the race issue in its external and most obvious form. In this phase it is constantly before the public and is perpetually used by leaders of both political parties. But, if this is the most obvious, it is far from being the most important aspect of the race question. What then is the race conflict viewed on its political side?

In the first pages of this chapter we emphasized the truth that difference of race is accompanied with lack of sympathy between those so differing. Ancient history and modern history agree in this dictum. The truth is as wide as human life. The white man in the United States has never shewn any affinity for the black. On the contrary, they have claimed and claim now the rights and privileges of the superior. As a consequence they take to themselves the right of ruling and do not put the interest of the other on the same plane as their own. The fact is that both political parties have used the Negro as an inferior. Human equality, the good-natured theory on which both parties rest, in the case of the Negro has not been adhered to by either. This statement will be met by a counter assertion. It will be said that the Republican party has raised the Negro to political equality with the whites in this government and that the Democratic party of the South alone denies him this parity of rights. But, we will not take words or names for the realities of things. Admitting the truth that the Southern Democracy has opposed strenuously the political equality of that race, we shall go on to find that the Republican party has in effect done very much the same thing.

What has been the status of the Negro in the ranks of the Republican party? Why was he made to enter that party? What is his place in that party now? At the end of the Civil War it became apparent, perhaps unexpectedly to the conquerors in that struggle, that the destruction of slavery had not destroyed the Solid South. The old foe still lived; sectional antagonism still existed. The Democracy which had so long controlled the government began to gather strength again. It must be defeated and the South ruled by the victor. This object the Republican party sought to accomplish by placing the ballot in the hands of the Negroes. The ignorant slave, easily controlled, readily deluded, was made to become the ally of the party which had set him free. Of course, it was natural that he should have made this choice, if choice he had to make; but, it is quite inconceivable that he could have had any voice in the matter. Those who professed that he was now their equal assumed over his political liberty something of the power of the master.

He was, for the time being, really introduced into another kind of servitude. Liberty for him, that is for the great mass of his people, meant the liberty of voting the Republican ticket, and so he felt it to be. So deeply was this idea impressed on his mind that twenty-six years have since elapsed, and he is even now somewhat, but not completely, governed by its influence.[2] During these years his place in that party has been that of a political menial. His vote has been used as far as possible to keep the party in power, but his interest has been lost sight of. He has been, one may say, encouraged to become the public enemy of the whites and has suffered accordingly, but his sufferings for which his party is largely responsible have not counted for much. Place, power,

[2] The "twenty-six years" which Seabrook refers to is the time which had elapsed since the Constitution of 1868 went into effect.

office, his white allies have naturally kept for themselves and left him the barren reward of bearing the burden of the fight. The white men of the South have used the Negro as a slave in the old days and made him work without adequate reward; and, the Republican party of the new days has also used the Negro, made him do their political work, endure the odium and ill will which he thereby suffered at home, also without adequate reward. In its general aspect, then, the race conflict on its political side, just as in other respects, is simply the contest of the white race against the black. It is independent of party names or passing issues. It is not confined to the South, nor is it only shewn by the Southern Democracy.

But, there is a more local phase of the political issue. The Southern whites are opposed to the exercise of power by the Negroes because in the first instance they believe that the great mass of them are unfit for such action, and further because they have in politics so long assumed a hostile position and voted with one party. It is against the Negro vote as solidly Republican that their opposition is directed, while the Negro on his part suspects the Southern whites and their intentions in regard to him. The causes of this antagonism are open to all. The Republican party in the struggle for power has used the Negro as a weapon of political war.

In one way and another, designedly and sometimes unconsciously, that party, particularly during the period of experiment and re-construction, has persuaded, deluded, and in effect trained the Negroes to be the blind foes of the Southern whites. The hostility which the Democratic party feels for the other it transfers to the Negro, the tool of that party at the South. In the meantime the poor Negro, who looked on during the war and never put himself in the position of an antagonist of anyone after it, has been be-tween the hammer and the anvil. As the helpless ally of the Republi-can party, the benefits he receives are very unreal, for it must be admitted that the right to vote for a very large number of his people is a very fanciful good; while, as the declared political foe of the people among whom he largely derives his bread, his un-natural attitude brings upon him ill will, sometimes hardship, and a lack of sympathy which might otherwise exist.

The difference of blood, the laws and sentiment against inter-marriage, the difference of daily work, and social position, all tend to make of the Negro vote a unit; and, it will probably remain so whether they take the Republican or Democratic side. This tendency to race solidity inevitably brings about fights between race and race at elections, sometimes with bloody results. But, considering the causes at work and the means used to bring about such troubles, one is filled with surprise that these things do not happen oftener and with worse issues. If the antagonism of the Negro to the whites were vital and sharp, irritated as he may be supposed to be by the interference of the whites, by the tricks used against him at elections, by the suppression of his vote, and stimulated by leaders of the meaner sort who would use him at all costs, riots at elections would assume very serious proportions. That they have not done so and the fact that of late years they are decreasing seems truly wonderful and speaks much against the race conflict idea and in favor of the natural good will of the people.

Consider the impulses to riot that are brought to bear upon them. In the first place, they recall long years of servitude. The evils of that period are magnified by the mirage of the time which has since elapsed. They are by no means certain that the days of slavery may not return. They see that despite the war the whites act in concert, that they consider in all things their own advantage, and that the interest of the Negro nation is not made prominent by them, be they Southerners or Northerners. And, as to that matter of slavery, they are in the bottom of their hearts distrustful of the white race. They regard their work as essential to the South; and, it is by no means clear to their minds, shut up in their narrow sphere of life, that the whites are really agreed that slavery is not a great advantage for them. When a Southern man asserts that he would not re-enslave them if he could, he will be greeted with a smile of silent doubt, the reflex of how many things they have seen and endured. That smile says, to him who knows how to interpret it, "I don't wish to call you a liar, 'boss,' but I know better than that."

It is to this deep-seated suspicion, this abiding fear, that the agitator appeals in addressing Negro crowds, not to their intelligent interest in other issues; for, if he does, he will appeal in vain. But, when he recounts for the hundredth time how the Government and the Republican party fought and won the war over his old masters and how certain it is that the Southern Democracy if it is able will re-enslave him and rob him of his little farm and clapboard shantee, he is enchained! The Republican ticket he will vote, he must vote it, he may even fight a little for it, and then his duty is done: the danger is warded off. And, tomorrow he appears with smiling face among the whites who were so formidable the day before and with shining face sets about earning his week's pay.

Conflicts at elections have been decreasing in number as the Reconstruction period and its fierce passions have moved away in the distance. The nation has had Democratic administrations. The Southern states have passed into home rule. The whites have not offered to re-enslave the blacks. They have kept up the public schools intended mainly for the Negroes' benefit. They have not robbed them of their property, have not passed any laws to prevent their earning full wages as they once feared, nor in any harmful way tried to curtail their energies. The chains which they were so often told that the Southern Democracy were forging for them have never been either forged or riveted on. And, on the whole, it begins to appear that the casting of the ballot is no longer as essential to their life and happiness as it once seemed and certainly not worth shooting another or having one's self shot for. All these things he sees, and, if he has lost interest in politics, it is largely because he has found by twenty-seven years of experience that both parties have a great willingness to use and cheat him and that transient political issues are not vital to his life and happiness, while peace and the quiet of his section very markedly are.

There are other and strong causes at work which tend to lessen the active interest of the Negroes in politics. When freedom first came to them, it meant in the minds of the great mass of the race "no more work." They did not clearly realize that the great value of freedom lay in the increased opportunity of working and with better results to themselves when freed from the control and greed of others. It was not so clear to their minds that money was the reward of toil and could not be created and distributed by government, or that the value of labor was fixed by what it could produce. All this they had to learn. The greater part of them did not realize that liberty is a delicate plant, which in order to be kept alive must be tended and nurtured, even when planted in a suitable soil, and that it depends upon the people who enjoy it and not upon outsiders to preserve its existence. Many of the great and imaginary benefits which they expected from possessing the rights of the citizens, from the very nature of the case, have not been realized.

As regards the Southern whites so lately conquered, they have seen them resuming their influence in the councils of the nation and men from North and South engaging together in business and social relations as though no great struggle had lately occurred between them—that an affiliation of the white people of both sections is possible despite the war and the differences of politics, at least, far more possible than an affiliation of the whites of either section with them. The consciousness of these facts tends to repress in their minds any latent desire, supposing the desire should arise, to assume a position of active antagonism to the whites. Their observation of events which may effect [*sic*] them is much more acute than is generally supposed. They are perfectly cognizant of the fact that their position and destiny in the United States is a national and not merely local question, and that they are contrasted with the white race and not merely the Southern people. They know thoroughly what race distinctions are and exhibit constant proofs of the existence of race prejudice among themselves. The mulattoes they look down on as being of mixed blood and assert race purity among themselves with some pride and distinctness. And lastly, the claims of superiority which the whites set up in regard to them are things which they thoroughly understand.

One must have lived among this race some period of time and have gained their confidence which they are usually slow to give in order to understand their ideas. And, having so lived among and seen them, he would be surely led to believe that it would require a brilliant leader indeed, and one able to offer great rewards, in order to move that race to wage any kind of active conflict against the whites, and to do this with an object of asserting race supremacy or getting control of state governments—achievements which at the very best could be of only vague or uncertain benefit, but would rather involve them in very certain disaster and place them in a false position before the country at large.

As a race they lack the mutual good faith in each other needful to organization; cunning is developed to so great an extent among them as to destroy their confidence in each other. And, moreover, they lack leadership. The Southern white man will not occupy that position for them, even if so desired, as against his own race; and, those whites who from time to time do assume this place, either from disaffected personal motives or philanthropic sentiment, have their work rendered arduous not only by the character of their followers, but also from the risk of losing credit among their fellows. On the whole, then, we are inclined to say that active political conflict on their part is very much of a myth. They are still largely the children of the past. What that long period of mental inaction and humility has been we all know, but we do not realize. The people of the South have made many mistakes about the Negroes. They have been too ready to forget that they have been swayed by a war party naturally unfriendly to the conquered section, and they have been too willing to visit upon these ignorant children of nature the faults of those who controlled their actions. And, the politicians of the North have been still more ignorant about this people. Their rigorous and self-assertive black "allies" at the South are neither as vigorous, as self-assertive, or as stupid, and by a long distance not as hostile to the white people of the South as they have believed them to be.

They have not the intellect, the means, the organization, and more important than all this, they have not the desire to carry on an active opposition. It is not at all a self-evident fact, as most people seem to think, that, if they were encouraged in the exercise of the ballot at the South and if their votes were fairly counted, that race conflict or Negro supremacy would result—unless we assume that the act of voting would confer upon them natural faculties fitting them to rule the whites and the desire to do so, which now they do not possess. There is really no fact in their past history, no fact in their attitude today which warrants this conclusion.

"What!" I hear someone say, "What of the Reconstruction

period! the days of Negro rule, of vice, corruption, bankruptcy! the degradation of the whites, the carnival of corruption!" The reply is readily made. During that period of misrule the ill results came about largely from the fact that the Southern whites abandoned the helm, refused to steer their own tempest-tossed ships of state, leaving in disgust and humiliation the task to pirates and thieves whose tool was the Negro, afterwards to be cheated and deserted. The experiment of Negro suffrage was made at that time under the most unfavorable conditions which human infirmity could invent.

In this matter of political contest between the races here, a fairer treatment of the Negroes in political matters than they have heretofore received would tend to diminish the attitude of conflict, if there is any, and remove the cause of complaint, thereby remedying the supposed disease instead of increasing it. Unreasoning suppression of them is largely the cause of conflict; it is not the conflict which produces the need of suppression.

If their interest in public matters were intelligently encouraged instead of being stupidly ignored, if their vote were counted and not repressed or made small by technical inventions, the chief motive for that vote remaining a solid Negro vote opposed to Southern interests would be removed and Southern politics would gradually lose its character of being a struggle between races. It is needless to say that this course is not pursued. In order to oppose Negro supremacy we adopt measures to make them desire it still more. In order to destroy Negro interest in politics we follow methods which will make that interest greater still.

And, we do more, for the evil does not stop here. With the same end in view it is demanded that the Southern whites shall form a solid Democracy, be bound in the iron band of a single idea: thus putting off still farther the natural affiliation of South and North, preserving hard and sharp the sectional lines, preventing the coherence of the nation, and strangely enough ruling the political action of the South indirectly through the medium of the very race whom we are trying to drive from the arena. The remedy prescribed increases the disease, and it engenders other diseases rather worse. The course pursued is false, and it will finally fail, as the future will shew. It is very costly, for it is followed at the price sometimes of peace and always at the price of prosperity and material advance.

But, there is a kind of discord at the South between the two races that is much more evident to the observer than any of those mentioned. It has its rise in the administration of the laws. The Negroes are apt to believe that the laws and their penalties are aimed against them; and, that as between race and race, they suffer the greater punishments. This feeling in them is the direct result of the habits and conditions of life in which they have so long lived. It is only then proof of the truth that the making of a citizen out of a slave is the work of a long period of time. Rapid creation, even in our fast-moving age, still is beyond human power. So long have the consciences of the Negroes been under the control of the consciences of others, so little have they been used to determine for themselves what is right and not right, what is lawful and unlawful, and so little have they been used to act upon such knowledge that they have no criterion within themselves by which to judge of conduct, and the sense of moral responsibility is very commonly inert. It therefore comes about that a deed which in their eyes may be natural and justifiable, or at least indifferent, from the standpoint of the other race is worthy of punishment. They then fall into the hands of the law in many cases, not so much from deliberate ill-doing, as from moral obtuseness, simple lack of the moral sense. Therefore they cannot escape the feeling that upon them the laws are particularly severe.

This fact is well understood at the South, and its long recognition causes the severity of the laws to be greatly relaxed in their behalf. Policemen, trial justices, officers of court, and juries all perceive the fact that they are meting out justice to a people many of whom do not understand the nature of their own deeds. The vices of the slave vitiate the life of the freeman. The habits of the slave render the life of the citizen imperfect and often impossible of attainment. A tolerance of the whites toward the blacks, which is often hard to maintain, thus becomes one of the virtues of the Southern people: it is rendered necessary by the juxtaposition, the intermingling of two races, who in their ways of thought and feeling are unlike each other, under the same institutions and the same civilization. A simple uniformity in the execution of the laws is under the circumstances out of the question. In its application to the Negroes the law, in some respects, may be said not to exist at all. In other respects the law is rigidly enforced and sometimes accompanied with a feeling of vengeance. The whites raise no serious objections to the Negroes practising [sic] among themselves their own sentiments about the exercise and value of the private virtues, but they will not submit to have these ideas and sentiments applied to themselves.

When a white man's residence or property is the scene of frequent robbery by the surrounding blacks—or especially when a white woman is forced to receive the embraces of a Negro—the entire white population in the neighborhood is stirred by a degree of anger which is not readily appeased and which often oversteps the calm impartiality of the law. Acts of this sort are looked upon not merely as the deeds of a criminal, but of a savage enemy.

The same feeling exists toward the Indian who has committed forays upon the settlers in the West, or the Chinese who is a heathen and natural foe. This state of things is unavoidable, considering the differences that exist between the races. The Negroes, the Indians, and the Chinese are all living in a land which they have not settled, under a system of laws which they have not made, under a government which they do not direct, and in a society of which they are not a homogeneous part. They are all subjected to the ever-present pressure of a civilization which they have not built up, and they are not in accord with the feelings of that race which surrounds and controls them. In order that the Negro race, or any race, should be in sympathy with the laws under which they live, they should make those laws themselves. In this country that is impossible, unless the white race could be expelled. What the nature of those laws would be, it is useless to inquire. It is only sufficient to remark that under them, as expressing the ideas of the African, the whites would refuse to live.

This chapter set out by stating the general truth that there is lack of sympathy between different races. The general truth is subject to special modifications as applied to the relations of the whites and blacks here. We have all along found that it is the whites who most strongly shew this attitude, that it is they who are most moved by the feeling of race hostility.

At the South where the races have lived together by day and slept together by night, it may be supposed that the greatest affiliation would exist; but, in some respects, the facts deny the truth of the supposition. The whites have never made any move toward union with the other race. They have not intermarried with them. Considering the great propinquity of the two peoples and the easy morals of one of them, it is surprising how few mulattoes have resulted from union of white and black. The fusion of the races through marriage or even cohabitation does not seem to be one whit more probable today than it was prior to 1861. In other respects also, the whites have shewn no tendency toward coalescence with the other race. They, even the most ignorant of them, have not adopted their careless way or life or been at all influenced by their religious ideas. The habits, feelings, customs of the Negroes are all alike indifferent to them. They owe nothing to the Negroes which they may have derived from the influence of that race.

But with the Negro the case is very different. They have approached the white race in many and sometimes very curious ways. "Old Massa," the genius of the past, and "de white people," the genii of the present, they have accepted as household gods. They work like them; they dress like them, adopting the latest fashions and colors with a grotesque imitation; they pray like them in their churches often with far greater fervor; they think like them, or accept their thoughts as the dicta of wisdom and like others to think that they are white people in all but color. They are by far the most imitative people on the face of the globe. That fierce sense of race individuality which belongs to other races of savages does not belong to them. The desire of resistance to others is not one of their traits. Did not the white race maintain hard and sharp the barrier against race fusion, the Negroes would willingly intermarry with the Anglo-Saxon and consider their status in life raised thereby.

The animosity between the races is very much less than one would imagine, if his opinion were formed by the constant use made of that theme by politicians of both parties. Fortunately, the Negro is not so easily spoiled by politicians now as he once was, and as time goes on he will be more and more difficult to use as a blind and stupid tool. The degree of peace which exists at the South has its sources in the following causes. The Negro's admiration of the white race is one of them. The natural friendliness of the Negro race is another. They do not seek out opportunities for discord or make occasions for quarrel. There is another factor as effective as either of these. It is the fact that the Southern people, so long used to live [sic] among them, have acquired that judicial and patient habit of mind which—beginning with constant restraint of oneself—gives control of others also.

These things more than the laws are the secrets of peace at the South. These are the springs of the strange power exerted by a handful of whites over a multitude of blacks. In fact, the natural relations of the races during the days of slavery now make of the whites the advisers, the teachers, and law givers of the blacks. The whites could not escape this position if they wished. Their ignorance, lack of self control, and foresight on their own behalf or on behalf of anyone else compel the whites to assume this duty. The fact is that the Negroes erect the whites into this position. As the electric lamps of the city swinging idly in the air only glow with light and usefulness by the power of the central works, so do the motiveless masses of the South derive the power of organized work and the principle of intelligent effort from the thought and conscience of the other race.

3

Remedies

It has been proposed to export the Negro race altogether, to remove them to Africa or the West Indies, the expense to be borne by the General Government. This remedy is based on the claim that the black race has always been an injury and misfortune to this country. That as a slave his presence produced more harm than good; that he was a costly laborer and had the effect of checking the growth of white population and emigration to the South. That more especially, as a freeman and citizen he cannot become a real part of the population. That he is a disturber of the peace and the source of an insoluble and endless problem—the cause of antagonism of North and South, a constant temptation to one party to use his vote to oppress and humiliate the other, and on the whole a source of dissension which retards investment of money, material progress, and peace.

Taking for granted that the evil cannot be ameliorated or removed, the remedy proposes to get rid of the cause by sending the race out of the United States. It is in its nature an appeal to force and a confession of inability to deal with the trouble in any other way. In the early ages of the world, when war was the business of life and peace a period of mere stagnation, when the noble-minded conqueror wept because he had no more worlds to ravage and reproached himself with tears for his unworthy inaction,

87

when cities were to be sacked and rich lands seized from their possessors, it was the usual habit of the victor—in fact was often enjoined upon him by a convenient divine command—to destroy, to reduce to slavery, or expel the inhabitant of the conquered country. But the nineteenth century, as it gazes at the long red track of blood which precedes it, looks also future-ward and dreams of better things, of an ideal of peace and humanity, an ideal which is not without power because it is not always realized.

There are strong moral reasons which will awake and be heard in the conscience of many [as to] why this race should not be expelled, for expulsion and nothing less it would be. It would tear them away from their old associations and the civilization to which in a great measure they have become attached. They would leave behind them their little possessions and the arts and industries which they now use, moreorless successfully, and subject them to a new life, largely among savages and uncultured wilds, and practically destroy the race improvement which they have reached in this country.

But, there are other reasons, not of a moral nature, why the proposal to remove the race could not be carried out. They have been made citizens by the laws of the land, insofar as the passage of laws could make them so. This being the case, their going depends on their own action in the matter and cannot be peaceably effected without it. They have acquired property in some states and could not be forced to quit or sell. But further than all this, the whites do not wish them to go. The Southern people, while they may not and do not value them as citizens, do value them as laborers. They act on the belief that the evils of their citizenship are fairly offset by the benefits of their work and their great adaptation to large parts of the South.

But lastly, the Negroes themselves do not want to go. They are no longer mere African savages. Some of them have achieved independence and respectability and have the good will and respect of the neighborhoods in which they live. The great body of them feel quite secure and "at home" in their position as laborers and servants and would smile, perhaps with confidence, at the idea of the "white people" being able to live without "de niggers." They consider that they have a hereditary right to do the work of town and country and draw the pay. White labor and the Irishman are their natural foes, and Chinese they regard as simple intruders. The enterprises of the whites, their methods of work, all the tools and implements of industry, and also the very climatic conditions of the South have become so interwoven with their daily lives that any movement looking to an abandonment of these could meet among them only opposition. No, the remedy of removal has no merits. Let us say then that the Negroes are in this country to stay. That here in a better clime than the fever-laden air of Africa, away from the daily struggle of savage life, stimulated, even forced forward by the leaven of the white race, adopting as well as they may the two thousand years of European civilization which surrounds them, they shall remain and live and work out their own destiny to whatever ends the laws of race progress and surrounding conditions shall lead them.

Will education remedy the present evils and those which are likely to arise in the future? The writings of the fathers of the republic all bear testimony to the truth that diffusion of knowledge among the people is the great safeguard of society. Statesmen, thinkers, and writers on economics all point out the same truth. It is recognized on all hands that, especially in a republic, majority rule may easily pass into majority despotism and opposite parties be easily ruled by warring demagogues unless the people are fortified in their public actions by a correct understanding of their institutions and governed by intelligence and morality. All these teachings are true, but do they apply in the present case?

If the opposition of the whites to the Negroes were based on the fact that the Negroes are ignorant and unlettered, then would the way be plain, then would the increase and diffusion of education remove the cause of dissension. But, this opposition is not based chiefly on the black man's ignorance. For other and more complex causes enter into the result. The whites antagonise [*sic*] the Negro because he is not one of them, because he cannot, from their standpoint, become one of them, be he educated or not. If he be educated, their disposition is that he shall exercise his knowledge among his own race. The white further antagonises the Negro of all degrees of education, wealth, or color, be he black or partly so, because he is of an alien race reared in the land of the whites as a slave without the wildest dream of his ever being here as a freeman or a voter, and because the victors in a bloody war which drained their wealth and destroyed what they believed their constitutional rights—not content with reducing their states to the condition of conquered provinces—not only forced them to accept defeat which they were ready to do, but further adopted the policy of controlling the states through the most humiliating of means: the ballot in the hands of their former slaves, by means of a race who, in their opinion, possessed by birth none of the qualities which the conquered were used to admire or obey.

The white opposes the Negro in public matters because they propose to hold the offices themselves and do not believe that the black race, from the very nature of the case, will exercise power or office with any regard for the good of the whites, or even of themselves. The whites all over the country object to the Negro on physical grounds. They will not join with him in marriage or intimately in social matters, with or without education, and tacitly assume in their conduct that all these antipathies are entirely beyond the pale of the law and that their attitude in these matters is entirely right and natural.

All these things may be called prejudices, pride, obstinacy, vanity. They may be so; but, in any case, it is to be remembered that prejudices are very real things, very potent powers in the life of each person and probably still more potent in the life of a society, and so grow by mutual sympathy. It is clear that the education of either race does not directly touch any of these things.[1]

The white workman, the mechanic, the farmer oppose the Negro[es] rather more keenly than the Southern man of the upper class because they come into direct competition with them. The feud on their part is of long standing. It is to be remembered that during the period of slavery the slave owner has ousted, has dis-

[1] In fact, by 1901 Albion W. Tourgée (whom Seabrook quotes later) concluded that education actually *strengthened* prejudice. Writing to President Theodore Roosevelt to congratulate him upon his controversial luncheon with Booker T. Washington, Tourgée said, "I realize now that . . . education does not eradicate prejudice, but intensifies it." Quoted in Edmund Wilson's *Patriotic Gore* (New York, 1966), 547. Wilson's book has extensive passages relative to Tourgée, Hilton R. Helper, George W. Cable, and others who have obviously influenced Seabrook's thought and development.

couraged, has kept down white labor, and has erected slavery over its head. That he has divided the state into two secretly hostile parts: the one of the slavocracy, the other of the non-slave-holding whites, and has controlled the state government in the interest of the former.

The Negro on his part also used to look and even now looks upon the laboring white man as a degraded creature and on the occasion of any personal quarrel does not hesitate so to express himself; while, on the other hand, he is open in his blind admiration of the "big white buckra" who does not work with his hands and in his opinion is therefore sublimely uplifted over his toiling white brother. One is often struck in a Southern city by the frequency with which one hears artisans—be they Northern or Western, be they Irish, English, or Scotch—abuse the Negro. Upon investigation the cause usually appears to be as follows. In many of the rougher kinds of work they find themselves underbid by the Negro who lives on little, wants little money, is easily & lazily content, and has no opinion of a white man who toils. Competition in work from their own race is a matter of course, but this damaging competition, coupled with a show of contempt and that from the race, fills these foreigners with ready and ill-repressed anger. And this is the case although they have not been reared in the prejudices of the South. The millenium is not yet with us; the ultimate perfectibility of man has not [been] reached. The ideal man has not yet burst the shell of human weakness and come forth all radiant with the light of heaven into our midst.

Education is not a specific against prejudice and evil passions. No people on earth can be pointed out where it has been so. From the period of the old civilizations when the Greeks calling themselves "autochthones," a peculiar people not derived from any other race, described the rest of the world as barbarians and guarded as a unit their society against the incursions of all outsiders, down to our period of civilization when the democratic West has expelled the Mongolian from their midst and refused him the rights of citizenship, the instance is hard to find where the superior (or one who so deems himself) stepping down from the place of power, which by struggle he has gained for himself, says to the weaker and the inferior, "Friend, come up higher." The world, whether intelligent or ignorant, has not grown up on this plan. Self-assertion, self-preservation, and egotism are inextricably intertwined with all the motives and actions of life. Being present in the lives of all individuals, they are still more prominent in the life of a society. But the inability of education as a remedial means of any great effect, except in the remote future, may be seen in the following considerations.

The work to be done is so vast. There is about twenty-five per cent of the Southern white population unable to read and write. Alongside of this, there is some seventy-eight per cent of the black population also illiterate. Great forests and tracts of humanity, as it were, are not yet claimed for civilization. These great masses of ignorance are part of the citizens of these states and may at any time become (and are at times) a source of danger to society. As a mere matter [of] self-defence, if for no other cause, these masses ought to [be] educated. And now arises the difficulty and in an unlooked-for quarter. Will they receive it? A man to be educated must toil in getting it. Study is not purely receptive. Minds are not empty jugs into which knowledge can be poured until they are full. The process of learning is equally [as] arduous as the work of the hoe or the plough, to many persons far more so and to even the most intelligent is far from being the amusement of a summer day. Into the grove of learning the most of us have been ushered, with not a few tears, by means of the rods cut from its boughs.

A man must desire knowledge before he can receive it. He must understand its uses; he must see the need of it in the affairs of life. Unfortunately this is not true of the Negroes of the South. With the mass of them the simplicity of life is too great; their occupations are too few and too simple; their circle of activity is too narrow; their connection with the life of cities is too infrequent and too incomplete to awake in their minds any due sense of the value of reading and writing even—to say nothing of the more extended education. The desire of education among them must go hand in hand with the improvements of their material condition, with better homes, with more diversified and skilled work, with better morals, and increased self-respect. There is no short method by which it can be made to precede these things, any more than rain can be produced from a dry atmosphere without the presence of clouds.

Let no one commit the injustice of judging the South by the standard of the industrial towns of New England. There the very employments of life are a school of mental and moral training. The division of labor itself requires a high degree of knowledge without which the earning of daily bread were impossible. There the school room, the factory, and the skilled specialties of the artisan go hand in hand. The gulphs [sic] which sunder the life of these two sections are too vast. The mind itself takes different views of life when inhaling the spirit of the two atmospheres.

The man who knows what the South is must become imbued with its peculiar life. He must be able to interpret actions without words and motives and methods without explanation. He must have drunk from that old gourd which hangs on the peg in the Negro cabin, the time-honored "kilbash," sat on the wooden chairs of plank and eaten hoe cake and pealed the roasted yam potato, must have attended those strange nocturnal shoutings kept up till rise of the morning star and hunted with dusky comrades amid the dense silent cypress swamps by the light of fat torches, guided only by the stars, for the abundant raccoon and opossum of that region.

He must have seen those strange midnight funerals by light of torches and been thrilled by the weird chants of the mourners; he must have perceived that feeling of content with things as they are and that fatalism which accepts evil and suffering as the will of God. And those malign influences, those ever-present spirits of evil! How real they are out in the lonely woods, how near and audible they become, how they ride in the gale and howl in the storm, how potent for life or death in the flooding and ebbing of the vast salt tides!

To the speculating person there is a strange fascination in these silent stirrings of the barbaric mind in which the primitive lamp of human civilization shews its first gleam of light. It is as though some infant consciousness looked out from its narrow cell upon the unknown, felt the presence of the great spirit of nature—the remorseless, the unchangeable, which is to be dreaded and propitiated, but not struggled with or explained.

The Christian religion itself has been poured into the mould of these ideas and been melted and fused along with their race conceptions, the result being that curiously blended emotional religion which now forms so precious a part of the Negroes' possessions. Disrobing ourselves of our personalities and laying aside our theories of one kind or another, let us as observers enter one of the "black rural districts" and look about us.

These then are their cabins, dotted here and there at considerable intervals about one of the old plantations. Many of them are hid in the low growth of scrub oak or palmetto, and only a blue line of smoke rising from the low chimney points out their location. The scrub oak and palmetto have grown rapidly of recent years in some of these localities. Most of these little huts are placed near the edges of the swamp or forest in order to be nearer the supply of firewood and water from natural springs. Most of these cabins have no window glasses; the chimneys are of crossed sticks made air tight with a mixture of moss and clay. The house is composed of two rooms divided only by planks or a calico curtain. In these rooms live one or two families in heterogeneous confusion. The intense heat of the summer pours down through the thin low roof; the frequent thunderstorms of this tropical section beat through the old shingles and splash over floor and beds. The winter winds whistle through the open walls and blow about the bed covers and the ashes of the wide hearths.

Small patches of farming land surround these cabins and in some cases belong to their inmates. They are not fenced. They are not drained. Small stagnant pools of water, "cow holes," remain from season to season. The children and women cultivate these fields; cotton and corn and potatoes are produced year in and year out. The natural loss of the soil is not adequately replaced by manures; and there is little evidence of improved culture. The system of tillage of the slave days remains in an imperfect condition, unaffected by recent advances in agricultural methods.

Many of these settlements are well nigh out of the path of the white man and seldom disturbed by his presence. Children grow up there in ignorance of the existence of a white race and scream with terror at his first appearance among them as if beholding an apparition.

These people have two sources of money supply: the one from

the sale of their small crops; the other and chief one from the wages made by the men in the various industries of the whites, if any chance to [work] exists within reasonable distances from these settlements. In what way, then, are they expending their money? Not in the building of better homes nor in the improvement of the lands. The same little comfortless huts remain patched up from time to time, the same unfenced fields and undrained ponds. The old spring is dirty still, only a few feet deep, and having fallen leaves still floating on its black surface. The same tumble-down cart and half-fed ox or gaunt mule are to be seen from season to season. In the meantime the brood of little dusky children increases rapidly and are soon large enough to seek their daily support either wading about creeks fishing or bringing sticks and brambles out of the thickets for fuel, or doing some light field work.

The entire earnings of these people pass through the hands of local white traders and are greatly reduced in the process. To these traders they look for every class of goods for use or adornment which they need or do not need from a pin to a coffin, from a pound of bacon to the decision of a personal quarrel. The goods which they purchase are usually of coarse quality and low grade, but they do not buy them at correspondingly low prices. The profits charged on goods are far higher than they ought to be in a healthy business; but, as the Negro establishes no supply stores of his own and waives all competition, he is compelled to accept the salesman's dictum.

After thus allowing themselves to be bound hand and foot in their money transactions, if only the proprietor has allowed them without rebuke to sit on his counters, swagger about his store, tussle among each other—and on some occasions with himself—they will trudge home Saturday evening over the long country roads lugging their supplies in high good humor with themselves and the storekeeper whose evident good will towards them appears to compensate them for the loss of their hard-earned dollars. As may be readily supposed, the worst foe of the struggling Negro race is the cunning white man of low tone, be he trader or politician. He is the vampire who sucks and never sates, and he it is who teaches the worst vices of the whites which are glossed with a more fatal attraction because the white man participates therein.

Thus the old trouble is constantly tending to reproduce itself. Thus there is possible a species of free slavery, this slavery of free ignorance to designing wit, cunning, and greed.

The towns in the agricultural districts present much the same picture. As in the country, so too here is the impetus towards the educational advance of the Negro not very great. The chief causes of this are: first, the character of work in those towns; and, secondly, the Negroes' lack of appreciation for education. These towns are usually nothing more than trading centres of the surrounding agricultural section. The skilled work is generally in the hands of white mechanics who are indisposed to competition with Negro workmen. The blacks are engaged in manual toil, demanding neither skill nor education of any sort, but rather physical endurance of fatigue, weather, summer's heat, and so on. Whether they can read and write affects very little their character as common laborers of this sort. And moreover, mere manual labor, toil of muscle, and daily sweltering in the fierce heat of summer of themselves—from a physical standpoint—act as deterrents among all classes of people from activity of mind and brain.

The other cause which checks their educational advance exists in themselves. It is a negative rather than a positive cause. It is not a savage opposition to knowledge, as may be supposed to be the case with the Indian, it is rather the absence of mental energy, the dislike of mental work, and a kind of stolid indifference to the means of improvement by which life becomes more intelligent and more perfect. They are too easily content. Life is with them too much a matter of today. The satisfaction of simple present desires fills out the sum of existence. Their mental eye does not look greedily toward knowledge as a means of ambition, as the great engine of their own progress, as the tool without which their participation in the life around them is impossible. They are too willing to let the white man, whom as usual they follow most trustingly in these matters, do the planning and the thinking. The habits of mind, which we are describing, are not anyone's fault. It is not the fault of the Negroes that they are a primitive and simple race, although they have suffered sufficiently therefor.

It is not the fault of the whites that the Negroes' mind is not alert, quick, and ambitious. All these traits or lack of traits are simply characteristic of a partially developed people. Beyond this, which at present is certainly true, nothing more definite can be known. Whether the Negro race is an inferior type or whether his past record in history and present performance are only due to his long living amid very hostile physical conditions and will improve with improvement of habitat, until he finally equals the white race as a people all these matters are for the future to settle. Time is the only philosopher who can decide them and results, not opinions, time will give.

And, the morals of the Negroes of one of these Southern towns. But we will not apply the word "moral" to the Negroes. It is not fair play to them to burden them with all the spiritual paraphernalia of the white race. Let us not say they are immoral, but say "unmoral." Whatever theory of morals the white man may claim for his own guidance, they do not feel that they are immoral in his sense of the word. When a man of fairly good character does a wrong deed there frequently arises in his mind a sort of double consciousness—a sense of the contrast between what he has done and what he ought to have done, and a feeling of regret perhaps springs up. He sees the ill effect of the bad deed on self and others, and he also sees the better effects which would have attended the better deed. Some feeling of self condemnation becomes prominent.

But, on the other hand, when one commits a deed without any sense of contrast between right and wrong, when he follows out momentary desires because they exist strongly within him as heedlessly as he would drink when thirsty or eat when hungry, these actions, however adapted they may be to attain the immediate satisfaction of present needs, are not to be classed among deeds moral or immoral. This tone or lack of tone of mind among the Negroes has forced itself more or less vividly upon the attention of all who have lived among them. It has had the effect of discouraging among the whites a belief in their ability for improvement. But we are judging him and his actions from the standpoint of the whites. What does he, the Negro, think and do about it? Is he, the party most concerned, filled with despair over his conduct? Not at all. The men and women of his race, after living lives and pursuing conduct which if suddenly introduced among the whites would destroy society, fill the jails and overflow the morgues, still go on their way with shining faces, overflow with good humor, increase and multiply, enjoy all manner of jubilee and religious gathering in total unconsciousness of those evils which to the white man and white woman constitute the essence of depravity.

Passing now from the realm of general statement, we will take our stand on the streets of a Southern town. It is the dusk of evening. The fierce heat of midday has given place to the sultry air of the night. The brick walls are still warm to the touch of the hand as we saunter along. Crowds are collecting in the streets, pouring out from all the bye-ways and alleys carelessly jostling each other and forcing us by sheer weight either to step from the pavement or be buried in the dusky mass. It seems to us that there are about twenty blacks to one white in this crowd which is composed mostly of females and children. Chatter in various dialects is incessant. We do not understand what they say, unless we are bred among them.

Oaths, coarse recrimination, and compliments of doubtless import are in fashion and are bandied in low tones from one side of the street to the other. But from long habitude we pay little or no attention to all this, scarsely hear it in fact. "They are only Negroes," we say and pass on in heat and dark distress with the odor of the surrounding human mass, very much unwashed and ill dressed, in our noses. The policeman is, or seems to be, on the alert and now and then makes a valuable capture of some little urchin or bootblack who perhaps has been "taking" fruit or coppers; for, perhaps his work that day has been unsuccessful and he fears to go home without spoils of some sort to appease maternal wrath. Paternal anger he does not fear, probably having never seen that relative.

Who are these children? The question is not easy to answer. Very many of them are illegitimate as we, with our artificial ideas of morality, would say. But, for them it does not affect their position at all. They stand on the same ground as those who come of married parents and, in fact, seem to care nothing about it. And who are these women whose shining faces are so full of good humor? A very large proportion unmarried, but still occupying all sorts of relations with the other sex. Many of them have changed their male partners since last year and will soon do so again. Some little quarrel on small pretext or perhaps a beating administered by her lord and the tie is relaxed. Man and woman go each their own way with wonderful self-content and flexibility and drift as circumstances favor into new relations or resume old ones that have previously existed. In matters of this sort they pursue their own happiness in their own way with comparatively little regard for the laws or morals of the whites which do not seem to apply to their case.

And, where are the men who do most of the work in this town? If it is near the end of the week and hence pay day, too many of them will be found in the rum shops and gambling dens of the dark side streets. They are giving away their week's wages. Full of pride at the shining dollars in their pockets, they are drinking, bragging, and "lawing" amongst each other over multitudinous bars. They are happy as lords now. They contemn money and will make more easily next week. As to the future, that is the business of God. At present they are swilling villainous rum from glasses designedly made half an inch thick. They are probably paying four hundred per cent interest on this liquor, but to all appearances are getting a thousand per cent pleasure from the indulgence.

This will go on with many of them until Sunday night; and, on the following Monday morning they will present themselves for work and ask their employer to advance them money in order that they may be able to live during the coming week. The politics of these bar rooms are of a kind with the liquor: abundant, well watered, illusive, and destructive. There is a straight passage leading from each of these establishments to the penitentiary whose doors are always yawning for new victims of bad whiskey and ignorance.

In dealing with this class of the population the law tends to become rigorous in its application. And how does the Negro feel toward punishment by what he considers the white man's laws? Very often indifference and sometimes contempt. After emerging from the jail or penitentiary, he resumes his former position among his people as though he were only an innocent and unfortunate person. "The state has been feeding him" as he calls it. Moral reform is not the result of punishments by a system of laws with which he is not in sympathy, and it is difficult to see how it could be [otherwise]. To what do facts of this sort point? Simply to the working of that natural law by which every creature, whether a man or a polyp, suffers when living amid conditions which it has not arranged for itself and to which it is not completely adapted.

The Negro is living in a social habitat built by the white race and to which he is not yet fitted. It is not true and it is not the intention to include in this foregoing survey all the Negroes of the town or country. There are among them, or rather by the side of them, a minority who are educated, intelligent, and respectable. Many of these are the descendants of families selected years ago by their owners on account of their good traits and who have been trained for several generations as body servants, domestics, and friends. The tone which they acquired in contact with the most refined element of the South, the mental breadth, and better habits still remain with them and their children, sharply dividing them from the rising generation of blacks. The children of this class and the children of the mulattoes form the best part of the pupilage of the public schools.

So far we have purposely excluded the mulattoes from our survey. They are properly Negroes, the law to the contrary notwithstanding. They neither think, feel, nor look like the blacks. This class offers a very interesting field of study to one who, taking the view of the naturalist, would see what heredity and fusion of blood can bring about. In them we have well cut features, thin lips, and often a very dazzling beauty in place of heavy features and clumsy limbs; intelligence and lively fancy in place of stolid and inert minds; a ready power of acquiring knowledge and ability to use it; and, together with all this, a display of the vanity and self-esteem of the white race. Their methods of work, their use of money, their homes, and their creed are all in contrast with those of the blacks. How have these results been achieved? Not by the century-long process of race growth, nor by inventions of legislation, nor by school houses, but simply by the fusion of the blood of the superior race, the magic potency of which has called forth humanity out of savagery—one may almost say, spirit out of matter.

The existence of this mixed race and its unhappy status in the eye of the law as a Negro has been a powerful factor in the black man's behalf before his freedom and since. If ever a harmonious juxtaposition of the races here would be worked out and a peaceable life of such discordant elements side by side be possible, it must owe its accomplishment very largely to the existence of this racial bond, which partakes of the nature of each race and owes blood kinship to both.

It will be remarked in the preceding pages that instead of discussing education proper as a remedy for the Negro problem here, every other phase of the question has been touched on. This has been designedly done. The spelling book and public school are very indirectly concerned in the matter. The fact that a human being can manage to read a name on a ballot does not mean that he will have any idea of its value, nor that he will feel interest enough to cast it, nor that he will do so wisely: otherwise the mere act of voting is a power of evil. The traits which make a citizen and a good citizen spring out of the society of which the man is part, out of the life which he leads, out of the habits of mind that life engenders. Hence have we been led to ask not so much can the Negro read, but what sort of society is that of which he is a unit? What kind of life does he live? What is his work? What is the habit of mind which is the outcome of these conditions? All these elements enter into the education of the citizen, for it is as a citizen that we are regarding him.

The education of the race must go along hand in hand with the growth of the South, with its material advance, with increasing division of labor which demands increasing intelligence, with more numerous industries, with more and better wages, and with the resultant improvement in his mind, his morals, and his self-respect. There is no conceivable way by which a society so imperfect as his is can be made to bring forth but imperfect results, except by a gradual betterment of the conditions on which that society rests.

Happily for all people of all colors and parties, the material growth of the South has begun with some vitality. The country has gradually awakened from the stupor of defeat and determined to live. It has shaken off also some of the apathy of the plantation ideas. Mills and factories, mines and furnaces, and railroads are springing into being. The smoke of tall chimneys, the buss [*sic*] of many spindles, and the long scream of the locomotive are seen and heard all about the waste places of the land. Southern ideas are changing, and the owls of the Middle Ages are being driven from their ancient covert.

In the meantime, while other causes are bringing about an improvement in the Negroes' condition with that of the country at large, there is every reason why the General Government should exert its money power in the extension of the public school system. Although a great part of the people are hard to reach, it does not follow that a rigorous attempt to reach them should not be continuously made. As a public measure it is and ought to be infinitely removed above all party politics. Unlike political issues in general, this question has but one side. The American people are concerned in it. Intelligence, even when it must be dearly bought, is cheaper than the continuation of ignorance which is supposed to cost nothing.

It may be contended that the measure is not constitutional, that Congress has not the power to make appropriations for educational uses and especially where the funds will be expended largely in certain localities and in certain states. But, the United States Constitution is not a fixed quantity, not a crystalization of powers: on the contrary, it has been adapting itself to changing needs; and, there can be shewn no sound reason why it should not clearly include within its sphere the right to apply its resources to a new fact, one which is at least as important as any that has come to the front since the foundation of the government.[2]

[2] Seabrook had apparently followed closely the public debate on the Blair Bill (1881–90). Senator Henry W. Blair, a New Hampshire Republican, actually proposed four different bills embodying the general concept of federal aid to education on the basis of the illiteracy rate in each state. Although some of these measures passed the Senate, none were formally introduced in the House. Bourbons such as Wade Hampton vigorously backed these proposals, but agrarian Democrats tended to oppose them, emphasizing traditional states rights and low taxes. See Allen J. Going, "The South and the Blair Education Bill," *Mississippi Valley Historical Review* (September, 1957), 267–90. In 1888, the Charleston *News and Courier* under Dawson favored the bill, but, by the fall of 1889 under a new editor and with Republicans in control in Washington, that daily said such measures smacked of federal control. If senators voted for federal aid (and control) of education, then to be consistent they would have to back federal control of elections! On

"Only give the Negro a white man's chance," say some, "and we shall see what he will achieve." This is the proposal of a philanthropy which, while it overflows with good intentions, yet, when viewed more closely, rests on a foundation which is largely an assumption. What is the assumption which is insolved [*sic*]? This, in short. That the opportunities, the means of advance of one people can be adopted by another people just as one would put on a suit of clothes. How has the white man reached his opportunities? Have they been given him by an omnipotent donor? And, has he found them ready-made and nicely fitted to his needs? By no means. He has painfully built them up as the oyster builds its home by gradual accretions from the insignificant little speck which the microscope hardly reveals until it becomes the strong and solid shell adapted to the life of the creature which lives within it.

The white race, like others, has found no royal road to progress. It has been engaged in the work of making its "chance" for hundreds of years. Now backward, now forward, has been its advance through partial failure and partial success, nor has it yet reached its goal. Today its material surroundings, its social arrangements, and its laws are nothing more than the expression of its needs and necessities—and not a whit more or less perfect than the men who brought them into being, and moreover they are primarily adapted to the race which made them. The Negro is amenable, no doubt, to the same laws of natural growth; and, like the white man, his "chance" he must make for himself. There is no one who could really "give him" the "white man's chance" if he would. Society has no physical or spiritual lever to bring about this result. At present the Negroes are living alongside and among the whites. They cannot escape the daily, hourly contact if they would. They are free to adopt the methods, the ways of thinking and acting, the very life of the whites so far as they may, the real

---

November 6, 1889, the *News and Courier* said, "In view of the marvellous material development of the South during the past few years, and its constant growth in liberality of sentiment and in wealth, there has been no period since the close of the war and the emancipation of the negroes when the South was less dependent upon the bounty of the National Government for the education of its youth than it is to-day. The most intelligent friends of the Blair bill themselves say that the educational progress of the South has been phenomenal. The South is able to provide for its own schools."

limits being to a great extent the limits which are within themselves.

The white man's chances do surround them on all sides, but they
are there for the Negro to achieve. He has been living in a land of
some enterprise and business; he has not built Negro enterprises
nor business. He has been living among a class of fairly moral
people; he, as a general thing, has not become fairly moral, although
he has advanced beyond his ancestral condition. He has been made
a citizen by a powerful government, backed by a powerful party;
and, although opposed by a minority of whites, he has not been a
success as a citizen or kept his acquired citizenship intact. And,
what is the significance of all this? It means that the Negro is in
the midst of a civilization which is entirely the civilization of the
white man and not his own. To this he has had to adapt himself and
so far the adaptation is not complete. It is idle to lay the fault at
anyone's door.

The Negro ought to be "given" perfect political rights. And,
so he has in a way. But if he is not equal to them, how is he to
be given them in any perfect sense? By the constant backing of
the government and the use of force to be regularly repeated? This
is self-destructive for it subverts the freedom of the state and
the freedom of the voter himself. The rights of the citizen can
only be acquired by his acquiring the qualities of the citizen. The
process by which men become citizens of a free country, when they
do so become, is not a sudden reaction of the individual but a slow
growth in which inheritance plays no small part.

It will be objected to these remarks that they involve an un-
provable assumption; namely, that the Negro is by nature incapable
of development. Such, however, is not the case. The real claim
made as the result not of theory, but of observation, is that the
Negro so far has not reached the plane of the old civilization which
surrounds him, one of the causes being that the period of his
contact with that civilization has been too short.

Here is another remedy of like nature with the preceding. We
quote from Mr. G. W. Cable. "The complete emancipation of all
balloters from all impure temptation or constraint is the key to the
purification of the ballot." [3] So indeed it is. Nor would anyone

---

[3] George W. Cable, "The Southern Struggle for Pure Government," *The*

who is a well wisher of his fellows desire to see this day of emancipation delayed. Then would parties and politicians grasping at office, heedless of the welfare of the nation, agitators of the race issue, advocates of the spoils system, and the despotism of money kings who under a different name enact the role of medieval barons, disappear and be no more the curse of government by the people and of the people. He presupposes as the condition of this emancipation and purification nothing less than a regeneration of the whole people of the United States and a reform of the entire working methods of popular election. He presumes that the poor man who is often indifferent to his vote shall not be ready to sell and that the rich man shall not be ready to buy it. That the timid shall not be ruled by fear and the ignorant by fraud and cunning. It is clear that nothing less than a reform of the very habits of thought and feeling among all classes can bring about such results as these. But the writer has omitted to state by what remedy or spiritual alchemy this desired reform is to be effected.

Mr. Cable says further, "Let us cease bounty, condescension, and fraud, and shew mercy, justice, and human fraternity." [4] As a moral suggestion intended to kindle enthusiasm and good will nothing could be better than these remarks; but, if they are intended as a practical cure for the evils of which he is speaking, one may as well ask that the wolf shall treat gently the tender lamb, or seriously propose that rivers shall turn and flow uphill. At this moment most of us are living in the high light of Christian civilization, or at least we like to soothe ourselves by calling it so. Its peaceful radiance has fallen on us for two thousand years. It speaks of love, of universal peace and good will. It holds up an exquisite vision of human perfectibility. Self-sacrifice is its theory of action and human brotherhood its chief tenet. Surely the day of reform must have come!

But, what do we see? Standing alongside of it in its very rays and marked out in bold relief are the vastest armies of which history

---

Negro Question (New York, 1890), 117. Cable (1844–1925), a New Orleans-born Confederate veteran, astonished and shocked the South in the 1880's with views expressed in both the *Silent South* (New York, 1885) and the *Negro Question*. See Arlin Turner's *George W. Cable: A Biography* (Durham, 1956), now in paperback (Baton Rouge, 1966).
[4] *Ibid.*, 155.

gives the record. The camps and arsenals of the most Christian nations are glutted with the engines of war and death, and the modern world is ready for the most immense effort of force which has ever shaken the planet. Michael and the devil have not ceased their ancient strife; and, instead of an era of peace, the opposing forces have increased in multitude and means of brotherly destruction.

The same class of facts is seen in the life of any country. The era of peace is not at all ushered in. It is true that the entire plane of modern life has been raised by the spirit of Christianity and the power of the sciences in bettering the means of life, but even upon this higher plane there still exist clear and hard those antagonisms and enmities and causes of war which divide man from man, and class from class, and race from race.

The authors of what we have called the remedies of philanthropy would seem to look for some marvelous conversion of both races. The rather hard truth seems to escape their attention that internal improvement goes along only with external advance. That intelligence comes not from a life of quiescent stupidity. That good morals do not come from a life of savagery. They would seem to expect that antipathy must somehow become love. That the strong shall abandon the use of his strength, the cunning man his fraud, the recent slave his habit of secrecy and subjection and distrust. That political equality shall exist where there is no equality in any of the other relations of life. That states must or can establish free governments, a large part of whose population, of both races, do not shew themselves equal to the task.

The unphilosophical nature of these remedies arises from a neglect to base the remedies on an analysis of the facts in the problem. The premises are defective, not the argument. It is for this reason that an attempt has been made in these pages, not to find remedies, but to arrive at a correct analysis of the facts and causes which lie at the root of what is called the Southern problem. All the institutions of society—be they church, government, or laws—are nothing more than organized human nature at last, nor can they vary much from that human nature out of which they have arisen. If the people are savage, there is the simple and easy rule of force. The African king kills his subjects freely and covers the roof of his shanty with their skulls. This is the right exercise and proper symbol of his power, and his people understand and appreciate it. The skulls are there to be seen!

If the people are composed of greatly sundered classes, especially in a period of outside war necessitating strong government, there arises monarchy and aristocracy with its lower classes and serfs or slaves, as in the Middle Ages—a condition of things which history records for 1,800 years. During that period [this was] the normal condition of society, despite the presence of Christianity and the existence of a form of free government among favored classes. Further, if the people are of a highly civilized race surrounded by conditions favorable to freedom, living in a state of internal peace, free of foreign war, of the same general race, bound together by a common sentiment—as was the case in this country in early days—and inheriting the sentiment of freedom, then the experiment of government of and by the people is possible and probable. Even under all these favoring conditions, it has not been a perfect success in this country, for during a very memorable period popular government was replaced by the military rule of the stronger, the sword took the place of the ballot box, popular discussion was replaced by the voice of the cannon, and for a time the old system of force resumed its ancient sway. The government reverted to primitive methods.

If a people's institutions are the organized expression of their life and needs, what rational ground is there other than a lofty enthusiasm for supposing that a mixed population like that of the South, under admittedly unfavorable conditions, shall or can make and maintain that perfect product of an ideal society which free popular government implies? Is it not looking for too much? Well, then, replies the well-meaning optimist, the conditions must be rendered more favorable. This is the obvious answer, and it involves nothing less than some moral regeneration of the people of both races, an advance in wealth, in diversity of work, the growth of an education in citizenship from actual participation therein, an increase of the feeling of unity between the races which now only partially exists. All these results are to be worked out. They can not be imparted. It is the work of a century and a century of peace, and perhaps more than one. We have read of Minerva, how she sprung suddenly from the head of Jove, radiant and fully armed. Yes! But it was from the head of a god!

4

"The Solid South"

It seems to be a favorite plan with some writers to account for the different political ideas of the two sections, North and South, on the ground of a radical difference in the peoples who first settled them. We read that the Cavaliers settled the old Southern colonies and brought with them a tendency to government by classes and that the Puritans settled New England and established pure democracy to the exclusion of class.

While the explanation has a real historic basis, it fails in the very important respect that it assigns but one of the causes at work and that one probably the least effectual in bringing about the contrasts which have existed so distinctly. Due prominence is not given to the ever-present fact of diverse climatic conditions. For the further explanation, we must appeal to the sun, the great and ancient divinity. We of the modern world have robbed him of his divine title, but his power he still retains. Following the sun the Negro gravitated southward. There he was welcomed as the best laborer in a hot climate; and, for the opposite reason he gravitated away from the North. Thus a very marked division in the character of the population took place at an early day. No question of morality entered into this natural segregation, unless the rise and fall of the tides or the flow of the Gulf Stream can be considered as moral phenomena.

There thus grew up at the North a homogeneous population free of marked individual inequalities and standing on the same plane in private and public affairs. At the South there collected and multiplied a confused unlike crowd, characterized by immense personal contrasts, one of the most marked of which was the relation of master and slave. The growth of these sections carried them apart from each other in life and sympathy. The desire of preserving and extending its slave institutions, which were weak and at variance with the free states and with popular government itself, unitized the South. Politics became the business of its upper class. In this way originated the "Solid South." Slavery as a legal institution has been abolished, yet the Solid South remains. We are therefore to conclude that the existence of slavery was not the prime cause which previous to the war made the South a distinct section. Had it been so, the removal of the state of slavery would have removed the difference. Abolition removed indeed the enslaved status of the Negro race, but the race itself it did not remove, nor did it greatly change nor could it greatly change the moral and mental character of that race, nor wipe out those great differences between the whites and blacks on which slavery rested and without which it would have been an impossible thing. As this is the key which unlocks the Southern question and lays bare its interior, let us pause and consider it more carefully. It not only unlocks the past, but in great part also the present. The proposition is this: It was the character of the African race which made slavery possible; and, now since the era of freedom, it is still the character of the African race which prevents its absorption into the life of the South. Previous to the war the nature of the African horde found expression in the natural condition of servitude. Since the war it is still the nature of that African horde which has rendered possible those political features which distinguish the old slave states from the free states and clearly define the limits of the Solid South.

What then is the character of this African race which has furnished the handle for slavery? Besides the difference of race, it is the habit, one may almost say the *love of submission*, mental sloth, and absence of self-respect. It is this habit of tame submission, this negation of strong traits, which has been used by all peoples in his enslavement, and [it] is today counted on by those European nations who are dividing among themselves his native Africa. It is remarkable with what smiling quiescense he has looked on while parties in this country have been fighting over his status and his vote.

Let us by way of illustration indulge in a hypothesis. Let us say that the Southern people had been willing to have held in slavery a white race and that the slave race was Italians. At the suggestion we quickly reply the attempt would have been a failure. The Italian slaves would have resisted, would have used murder, force of arms. The cost of guarding them by night and day and the difficulty of making them work on that plan would have rendered the attempt abortive. It would not have paid. In fact, this white slavery would have cured itself. Not only would they have conquered freedom, but they would have achieved for themselves the sympathy and respect of their would-be masters, and finally have become an undistinguished part of the general population. It is needless to say that the Negro race before and since freedom has conducted itself in a very different way. Their submissive nature has furnished to the white man a lever by which they could be enslaved, and their incapacity has given him abundant excuse for keeping them in that condition.

There are further causes for Southern solidity besides those springing from the characteristics of race. The War of Secession has been fought. It issued in the fortunate result of saving the Union and giving reality to the national idea. It has transformed "we the people" of sovereign states into a nation owning a General Government. Then followed the puzzling period of Reconstruction and experimental legislation. The Southern whites and the lately freed Negro slaves were placed by law on the same civil and political plane. But the act of Reconstruction did not, because it could not, extinguish the passions of war; and, it further aroused the hostility of the Southern whites by conferring upon the servile class the power of an unqualified ballot. As frequently happens, the ball which had been put in motion did not stop at the intended point. The Reconstruction measures partly did the work at which they were aimed, but they also did other work at which they were not aimed.

Here is some of it. When the Negro was made a voter his vote was free. Theoretically he had the power and the right to give his vote to any party. Presumably he was not made a voter in order that he may give his vote to the Republican party alone; for, if he was gifted with the ballot solely on the condition that he should cast it in a certain way, then his liberty as a voter was a mere sham and his political freedom only a shadow. He was, in fact, only passing from one kind of slavery into another. What then did he do? Did he exercise the untrammelled freedom of the ballot? He adopted and still adopts, but to a less blind extent, the opposite course. He looks upon himself as the enforced ally, the political servant of the Republican party at all elections and on all measures. Blindly or not, for good or for evil, he votes only one ticket. Should the candidates be Democratic, should the measures proposed come from that party, they do not affect him and are without the range of *his* public affairs altogether.

The Reconstruction measures have done more than was intended. They have put the Negroes in a condition of political vassalage to one party irrespective of other consideration. The Negro has been under the influence of a purely partisan training, and he has been educated into the political enemy of the Southern white man. Although friendly disposed, often too much so, in other matters, yet in matters political he is, or thinks he is, the opponent of the whites. There has thus been little chance of his taking an intelligent view of public affairs.

This is another cause of Southern solidity, at present the chief one. This subserviency of the Negro to the Republican party works out in several directions and in most with unhappy results both for that party and himself. In the first place, it destroys the interest of the Republican party among the Southern whites and perforce places them in the opposition. It is by no means true that all whites at [the] South were really Democrats. The blunders and crimes of what is miscalled at the South the Democratic party, that is, the Southern oligarchy, are by no means hidden from all who dwell south of Mason and Dixon's line. The course of the Republican party in the matter of secession, the saving of the Union, the prevention by force of arms of a sectional division of the states by which untold future disasters were avoided, the lenient conduct of the government toward the conquered states, the fact that the property of the vanquished was not confiscated or their leaders hanged, even the attitude of the party on tariff measures which becomes more "constitutional" at the South as its manufacturers increase—all these acts and measures have supporters at the South as they are better understood.

But, the policy of that party and its practical result of educating by agitation and otherwise the easily controlled Negroes into the public enemy of the Southern whites has been too entirely destitute of statesmanship to awaken anything but a genuine hostility. This course has been destructive of the interests of that party at the South, and it has other ill effects. It is injurious to the Negroes themselves, although they in a blind adherence to what they have regarded a necessity have not paused to consider it. Climate and the character of Southern work, the abundance and cheapness of land, all conspire to keep the Negroes at the South. It is difficult to see how they could get away even if they so desired. Having thus their life destiny cast in the same land as the Southern whites, it is not to their interest to take a stand of hostility and blind distrust and to do this on no other ground than that "the party" so instructs them. To say the least, it is a very poor education in citizenship. It makes for them enemies among the whites who then look upon them as dangerous tools and who are apt in their daily dealings with them to exercise a degree of harshness and sometimes injustice from which otherwise they would refrain. The "Solid South" has helped to produce the Solid White South.

The Negroes' education as a citizen has been marked in both directions. By one party, unfortunately, he has been trained as a political servant; by the other, composed mainly of those among whom his lot is cast and whose interests are largely his own, he has been taught not to cast an intelligent ballot, but to regard his vote as a myth of no reality or account, a thing to be bought for a few cents or taken away by force or cunning, and of no moral account. He has been under poor schoolmasters. Both contending parties, struggling between each other, employ him as a weapon; both use him and delude him; and both practically deny him equality.

When the Negro succeeds in escaping from his condition of

party domination, throws off his present political slavery, and is ready and willing to cast his ballot for either Republican or Democrat or independent, then will his political value at the South vastly increase, then will he have escaped from that position blindly forced upon him of an unreasoning opposition to all the interests of one party and a perfect servitude to all the measures of the other. The "Solid Black South" will then tend to disappear.

Several conditions are essential to this result; and, it may be that most of them are yet distant. They presume nothing less than this: That the Republican party shall abandon its partisan policy in the Negro question; that the Negro shall become something more than the mere "ally" of that party; and, lastly, and far more important than either, that the Southern whites on their part shall cease their habit of making political foes of that race and substitute a policy of fair dealing.

We have been endeavouring to point out that there are three great causes of the "Solid South." We first emphasized the character of the Southern population, and we found it made up of very unlike elements, not apt to combine into a single race. We next found that the large Negro element of this population has been trained by the party who gave them the ballot into a position of political enmity to the Southern whites. And, lastly, we pointed out that the Southern whites of their own action have further increased the trouble by suppression of the Negro as a political factor. If these causes can be removed, the peculiarity, the individuality of the South as a section may be lessened, if not finally obliterated. As to the first, the difference of race, this is probably due to physical causes and laws of heredity acting through long periods of time. It can not therefore be directly changed by any known means, certainly not by any exercise of good will, nor by any legislation in the case. The only method which could effect immediate results, race intermarriage, is out of the question so far as any one can now see.

As to the second cause, will the Negro abandon, can he be persuaded to abandon, his subjection to the Republican party, rise from his position of political servitude, and vote as an independent citizen? We will not impugn the theory and motives of those who made the Reconstruction measures because the lately freed Negro slaves failed properly to appreciate them or work them out into good results. This course was to have been expected of them. It is only proof of the fact that a slave cannot be made a citizen by the passage of a law. The rights of the citizen found them largely unprepared. They naturally obeyed their new leaders with unquestioning confidence, to what ultimate result they did not know. They saw their old master class conquered in a great war. They knew that those who had freed them were the enemies of that class, and they felt that their old owners were opposed to their newly acquired rights. The vision of a possible return to slavery ever floated before their minds. There were other reasons for their Republican allegiance. Their fears influenced their actions, and that habit of docility and submission which they had been so long learning under their old masters they now practised under their new. They would not have dared to have acted otherwise. They went with the strongest party.

Is this analysis too cold? Is it mere pessimism to say that it was not gratitude which enrolled them on the Republican side? The Negroes expected from their newly gained rights all sorts of imaginary and impossible results. They had to learn by weary waiting that citizenship has no intrinsic value for any man unless he knows how to value and use it and that freedom from work and abundance of money are not given along with the ballot. They had, despite their citizenship, to meet the problem of life, not as slaves supplied with land and houses, but simply as a multitude of penniless and sometimes homeless laborers. And they began to look about them and to see that the change in their status which they owed to the Republican party did not of itself work a change in their material condition and perhaps, at first, in some respects made the life problem harder. The gradual perception of these things worked a disillusionment in their minds. The inevitable result has been that their interest in politics or in the only kind of politics known to most of them, that is, voting a Republican ticket, has been declining.

But, they learned from late experience more than this. They have found out that the white man who is a Republican is very much the same thing as a white man who is a Democrat; and, although of different parties, they are very much more akin to each other than either of them is to him. In short, that the white man assumes the superior claims of the white man independently of any political professions. He has come to see that when an election occurs he is valued on the ground that he can vote, after which his importance ends; but, that when offices are to be parcelled out, the white men manage to install themselves therein, as of natural right, until another election occurs and the same thing is repeated. This is discouraging, but also inevitable. It is the old thing under a new form. It is a change of name, but not a change of substance: the white man over against the Negro, accomplished by the results which arise from that unequal relation. The white man of all parties grasps and rules; the Negro yields and obeys. Thus, we are brought back once more to the general proposition with which these pages set out: that the entire relation of the races is the result of causes acting through long periods of time and for that reason is constantly repeating itself.

The Negro has been losing his interest in politics. Gradually as the years went on and his practical experience has grown, he has been abandoning his fealty to a party, which he does not himself appreciably influence, which he does not to any extent represent, to which his race furnishes no leaders, and which has no strong representatives where he mostly lives. His subserviency to the party is by no means so absolute as it was in the days when to his unused fancy it promised impossible rewards of all kinds. On the other hand, the dreaded monster, the Democracy, has made no move toward devouring him and his. A degree of quiet and peace has been attained throughout the country in place of unrest and uncertainty, which has given security to business, opened the way to work and pay, and made it possible for his hungry multitude to earn wages and homes and independence. His action in the matter is the best practical proof of what he thinks about it. He is, so far as one may judge, contentedly settling himself here. His race is more and more localizing itself at the South, despite emigration agents and despite the poor treatment he is supposed to undergo. The better class among his people is buying land and making homes and saving money. In all rights of the citizen which are not purely political they enjoy not only a freedom, but a license which is often inconsiderate of the comfort and rights of others. They are untrammelled by the restraints of sentiment and custom which the whites impose upon themselves and enjoy an amazing amount of race individuality.

They have gained in knowledge of men and the world and have come to know that their status in their party is one of subordination. They feel secretly in their hearts that the white race of all parties is a unit, be they Northern or Southern, English or German; and, they know that their natural affiliation is not with any white man's party. Does any one believe that they are under any illusion about their real position in the United States? To suppose that they are indeed attributes to them a degree of dense blindness which is proof against every experience of daily life and against the experience of the last thirty years in particular. Are they so dull as not to see, or to begin to see, that the Republican party has ruled them, not especially for the advantage of the colored man, but for the perpetuation of their own power? The fact is, they do see this, and in some cases say so. Therefore, we say that the Negro fealty to a single party is losing its former intensity. The political animus of the Negro, never very strong, is growing weaker.

There are a good many ideas, a good many wishes attributed by the whites to this people which they do not entertain. One of them is the desire for Negro supremacy. If instead of this we should say that what they really want, but do not distinctly confess, is the autonomy of their own race, free of white influence altogether, we should fairly hit the truth. This desire of race independence they do not readily confess. They think that if they were separated from the whites, occupying a separate locality or territory and holding a somewhat independent political attitude, they would then hold toward the whites, not a relation of quasi friendship as now, but one of hostility, and this position with its risks and difficulties they are not anxious to seek. They have no faith in the whites when the whites become even partial strangers. As to "supremacy" over the whites, they never dreamed of it! But, they do want some race emancipation, and they know that they have not attained that in this country. For the white race is still here in vast majority and, instead of living equally and freely with them, insists on distinctions of all sorts, and stands on the ground of superiority, and this broad fact is true over the entire country, and is not confined to the South.

Will, then, the Southern whites encourage them to act with themselves and take an intelligent interest in state as well as national politics? It is too readily taken for granted here that the case is hopeless and that the attempt would prove a failure, as it did in the early days of Reconstruction. But, the Negro has changed somewhat, and times and influences have changed a good deal since then. Let the truth be admitted that the black man is amenable to reason. That his race furnishes many individuals of intelligence and responsibility. That there is no reason to suppose that they naturally love bad government and corruption when not trained and forced into that course of action. Further, it ought to be recognized that that race is distinguished from mere savages by possession of very important qualities. Their docility and good will are very marked, nor have they as a people ever been hostile to the interest of the whites, except when made so by the action of the whites themselves or excited by shameless leaders. While, on the other hand, they are great admirers and imitators of the superior race, and their faith in any white man who shews kindly intentions toward them is indeed marvelous. These traits ought not to be regarded as only characteristics of good-natured animals, but valued at their true human worth.

Again, their quasi hostility to the whites during the Reconstruction era cannot be fairly cited as an example against them. We have pointed out that at that time they were slaves and not responsible for their actions. They were clay in the hands of the potter, and the course they followed was largely one of necessity. These considerations, these traits and characteristics of theirs all furnish a road by which they may be approached, a means by which a political unity of the races at the South may be brought about. Of recent years their political suspicions of the Southern state governments have been allayed. They know that by them they have not been injured, in person or property at least, and moreover have been directly benefited; and, led on by this knowledge, they have proceeded to establish themselves at the South. In the conduct of business they have found that the Southern man is neither harder or more dishonest than an employer from any other part of the country. All these things are causes which tend to bring about political harmony between the races, for a man's public sentiments and actions are largely governed by the simple influences of daily life.

The decisive step toward the real emancipation of the Negro, the strongest move toward his introduction into an intelligent exercise of the rights and duties of the citizen, must at last be made by the Southern whites themselves. The circumstances of the case have all along compelled the people of the South to elevate and improve the blacks, and it is very probable that the same set of circumstances will go on so compelling them in the future. The necessities of the case will ultimately force this line of action.

Will the Southern people come out of their ramperts [sic] and call a truce? Will they abandon the policy of suppression and encourage the Negroes in an intelligent use of their rights? Will they "risk" doing this? That there is such a "risk" is claimed by a good many people who think they know. That there is danger at the South of "Negro majority and Negro supremacy" is a general opinion, and it is probable that the opinion stands on good ground so long as the present hostile policy of the South continues. It is very easy to find enemies, a very simple matter to create foes. No other result than the compacting of the Negro vote into a solid unit could be expected; and, even though he should be prevented from actually casting it, the trouble remains because the motive and intention to be and remain a unit grows and nourishes itself. This policy of rejection, this habit of suppression makes fuel for the fires of disaffection. If then the dangers and the injuries which it is feared will arise from the Negro vote are to [be] escaped, the causes which are at work and which tend to make that vote both solid and hostile to the interests of the South must be removed. It is childish to hope that any final settlement can be reached in any other way.

And, what is the counter course of action which is proposed? It is this. Do away with those things which tend to make a solid unit of the Negro vote. Remove the impetus which throws them into an unreasoning opposition. Cease making fuel for the fires of discontent and suspicion; and, for the first time since their freedom, do what neither party has ever really done: Encourage them to take an intelligent share in the performance of the duties of the citizen. And, let the move be made by the Southern whites and at home, thus effectually barring out adventurers and partisans who otherwise would erect themselves into leaders of their credulous multitudes.

It is well to see that the difficulties in the way of such a course are very great. These difficulties are based on various antipathies, but chiefly on a great lack of faith in the Negro where the Negro is to exercise power. It is not easy to wipe out from the Southern mind the fixed belief that if the Negro citizens voted freely they would not straightway aspire to elect a black ticket, introduce an era of ignorance and misrule, bring about strife between the races, and render needful the establishment of military rule; and, that should this once occur, race politics would become the established state of things. That this would be the wretched outcome the whites are generally persuaded, and hence it is claimed that the two races here cannot exercise equal political rights.

It is argued that in order that there may be a peaceful equality of power the two peoples must possess a natural equality, which they do not; or, that failing this, the two peoples must exhibit an angelic temper and patience, the one to the other. And, that while a minority of each side may have such virtues, it is too much to hope that such qualities will be possessed by the opposing hosts. In order then to avoid all these complications, the white man says, "We will not allow the Negro an equal voice; we thus get rid of him as a political factor and, in so doing, avoid making dangerous experiments and destroy the certain source of trouble." This is one solution, apparently, of the question. It has the one great merit of consistency at least; but, as we have pointed out, it is weak in this respect, that it is purely temporary and staves off the trouble without doing anything to remedy it.

The other policy which we have been discussing is of a different and radical nature. It aims to remove the germ of the evil itself. It proposes not to pursue the method of suppression, nor to eliminate the Negro from politics; but, on the contrary, to accept them in such a way as to eliminate their need of opposition, for it is the hostile attitude rather than the man which may be the germ of the contemplated troubles. This has been the policy of those nations which have been the great civilizers of the world. When the executive genius of Rome spread its power over the barbarous nations of Europe, enemies were made friends, the conquered were made allies. Caesar, the soldier, was also Caesar, the statesman. Along with the eagles there marched a still stronger power, the spirit of a rational liberty.

It is claimed that if the Negroes were allowed political power they would again seize the state governments and reenact the corruption of the Reconstruction period. So argue most of the Southern leaders. But, as an argument it will not bear a careful investigation. It involves several assumptions which are not facts. It takes for granted that it was the Negroes who set on foot, devised, and carried out the corruptions of that period of crime. It assumes also that during the years which have since elapsed that race has become no better fitted for the duties of citizenship; and further, it would seem to imply that under better leaders and purer influence the Negroes would again follow the same course of conduct. It must be admitted that these assumptions are not so self-evident. It is not historically true that it was the Negroes who directed the Reconstruction governments. The deliberate crimes under forms of law, the ingenious frauds, and the acute scoundrelism of that epoch were the inventions of white men whose talent in that line seems indeed limitless. The Negroes were only the inexperienced tools used by these political "cracksmen." An intelligent choice they did not have; in fact, in their then position, no choice was open to them, either good or bad. On the contrary, every means of fear, bribery, and prejudice were steadily used to make and keep them the blind retainers of leaders whose interest ended with themselves and whose corruption was so great that one of their number has since said of them, if they were washed of their crimes it would be needful that they be anchored in the Atlantic Ocean.

During these dark days the usual fruits of war were being reaped. The army of officials who held the state governments was composed of camp followers, Bureau agents, politicians, and professional men who had failed at home, and Southern renegades of low type which the late struggle had brought to the surface of affairs. Under pretence of founding free governments at the South they founded schools of violence and fraud. In these schools and under these teachers the newly made Negro citizens were trained with the results that are so well-known. Elections were carried "with the bayonet at the heart of every rebel in the South." United States marshals and bodies of troops traversed the counties of every state in every direction. Constabulary forces were present at all the elections to intimidate the whites and concentrate the black vote. With the same end in view the blacks were formed into militia companies and kept under pay which was drawn out of the state treasuries. Crimes and acts of violence between whites and blacks were rather encouraged than repressed in order to make excuse for intervention of Federal troops and military arrest. All these measures and doings had the effect of coercing and controlling the Negro vote. There was nothing for them, so far as they could see, but to obey the commands of their leaders, and with the then ignorant blacks their wishes became law.

Nourished by all these conditions, race prejudice on the part of the hitherto peaceful Negroes tended to become marked and sometimes violent; and, it was encouraged by their white leaders because on its existence and on its results the power of these leaders depended. Negroes, on the other hand, who ventured to cast a Democratic vote were expelled from their churches or suffered acts of violence at their homes or in the public streets. In fact, the Negro citizens were bound securely in the desperate grip of a tyranny of vice and misrule while filled with the belief that they were to receive nothing but benefits and blessings. Negro members of legislature of course followed the lead of their virtuous white brethren, accepted bribes offered for their votes, and cast them in such a way that the white patriots pocketed the spoils. It is very clear that it was the genius of the white race, and not the Negroes', which presided over this feast. Such royal plundering was worthy of the Anglo-Saxon who despises small pilferings and mean jobs.

It is now nearly twenty years since that period of demoralization has passed away. Greed had exhausted the stores on which it fed. The financial credit of the South was gone. Business interests had suffered severely. The making of good state governments had not been achieved. The discontent of the people had passed the limit of endurance, and fortunately the long period of misrule had aroused the condemnation of thinking men all over the land. The evils of the time, at last by their very intensity, brought about their own dissolution.

During the period of repose, which has since elapsed, passion has yielded somewhat to reason. Both whites and blacks have had time to look quietly about them and take their bearings. A degree of quietude and some combination of interests have sprung up between the races. The season of peace has not been without its good effects upon the Negro population. They have had an opportunity of seeing for some years that a government is not necessarily a thing of soldiers and bayonets. That public offices are not created primarily as a means of robbing the people, and that an era of peace is needful for an era of prosperity. In the meantime their political education has also advanced. It is over two decades since they were made U.S. citizens and voters. They have ceased to be things and have become men; and, while in some cases freedom has been a burden, it has brought along with it responsibilities that have not failed of elevating results. They have been learning one of the first lessons of human rights, the right of honest toil to be paid for its work. Their freedom to engage in the affairs of everyday life, to employ and be employed, to buy and sell, &c., has taught them the lessons of a common justice.

The Negro as a citizen has greatly advanced of recent years; and, for this reason it is unlikely, in fact altogether impossible under the changed conditions, that he could or would again become the stupid and facile tool for wrecking the public prosperity and plundering treasures of state. But, there is another truth that it is well to remember in this connection. The fear of majority rule, either white or black, is a very fanciful terror. It is one of the evil spectres which are used to alarm and control the people. The control of government by the mass supposes an amount of unity and intellect that the mass does not possess. The fact rather is that popular government expresses itself in minority rule at last and assumes a very oligarchic character. Every enterprise, every organization, every piece of work that men do in common works itself out practically in this direction. Popular government indeed destroys the existence of titled classes and legalized power of birth, but the power of intellect, money, character, and their possessors it does not annul by one jot or one tittle. In this country the professional men, the holders of land, the great employers of labor, the owners of mills, mines, and railroads are practically the ruling class. In them inhere leadership and power as naturally as the force of gravity inheres in matter, and their influence controls the lesser social units that surround them. Strong and real indeed and based on very good reasons must be hostility between the multitude and the minority of wealth and knowledge to check the working of this common and natural law. It is against a course of conduct at the South that tends to organize and keep up this hostility that the preceding pages are directed.

Passing by the probability or improbability of such a course being adopted, let us suppose that the South abandon its past and present attitude and take not a backward, but a forward step. Let the Negroes understand that the whites are ready for a political truce. That the end to be attained is the repose of society and the general benefit of the people at large, of both races, who can not escape from each other and who are involved in the same failure or success. Let them be encouraged to interest themselves in local politics, to attend public discussions and elections, to vote less as machines and more as men, and to expect to have their votes counted. Let public prints make clear the fact that the voting of the Republican ticket is not a law imposed upon them by the U.S. government, not a prime necessity of life, and the Southern white man is capable of using toward them in public affairs the same justice and good will which he displays in private matters.

Among other objections, someone will say, "The attempt would be useless." "The Negro will never put faith in the Southern white man in politics." So be it. But, the bare attempt would of itself be a victory. Its immediate result would be to remove the colored man's suspicions and breach the wall of distrust. To the unquiet mind, fearing it knows not what, a chance to see is the greatest of all pacifyers. A flash of lightning in the night and darkness is a boon to him who sees not the road.

As matters stand at present and in truth as they have stood ever since the war, everything in the Negro's mind is necessarily uncertain. He knows not what to expect in this land where he feels much like a stranger. Unknown enemies surround him, and he gropes along suspiciously and mechanically. He tends to have an exaggerated idea of the value to him of political power. What else could be expected? The more he is denied its exercise at the South, the greater he fancies its value. Nor can he ever clearly see its actual import and know its limitations unless he exercises it in fact, unless we of the South claim that we will enact that bit of nursery wisdom which used to warn us that until we had learned to swim "we should not go near the water."

The fact is that there is no reason why they should not in political matters have the same faith in the whites of the South which they shew in other relations to so very marked an extent. And, the fact that they have not, or appear to have not, for there is much pretense about it, is directly traceable to the action of the whites themselves of both parties. It is high time for the people of the South to see this truth. As to this claim that the Negro will never harmonize politically with the Southern people, no one has the data on which to base it. He has never had anything like an opportunity, ruled as he has so easily been by one party and repelled, expelled possibly, by the other.

The Negro mind is highly secretive and retentive of its opinions and feelings. It broods a long time before it forms a conclusion and then, except under very encouraging circumstances, is apt to keep this conclusion to itself. Its motives are darkly locked up in the deeps of a consciousness which for thousands of years has been practising the habit of concealment. It is out of the power of anyone to assert that they would fail to act politically with the people of the South if the chance so to do were fairly and in good part offered them. On the other hand, the antecedent probability is very great that with the quieting of their suspicions they would transfer to the Southern whites even a greater degree of unreasoning confidence than they perforce yielded to the Republican party of Reconstruction days. But, unreasoning confidence on their part is not what the South ought to want. Unreasoning confidence in one party and unreasoning dread of the other is the trouble with them now.

It is time that this whole question, with its very serious aspects, should pass out of and *above* the arena of mere parties and politics. It is and has been too long a source of ill feeling between North and South. It costs too much from a moral standpoint. It is the occasion for abuse and recrimination. It furnishes the Southern demagogue and Northern agitator, both anxious to keep themselves before the public, a ready means to excite and delude the people. It renders hopeless a wise and rational treatment of national measures. The war, whatever its other results, has not settled this matter. Force is not the method. It remains for the South now, and moreso in the future, to work at the solution of this problem. There is no escape.

5

A Resumé

During the period of slavery the people of the South, in the usual acceptance of that word, consisted of the white race, the Negro slaves not forming a vital element of the population. At the end of the Civil War and as a result of that struggle, a great revolution took place. By the Thirteenth Amendment of the Constitution of the U.S., the entire body of slaves were declared freedmen; the Fourteenth Amendment raised them to the plane of citizenship; and the Fifteenth Amendment, ratified by the legislatures of the Southern states, declared the political rights of the Negro citizens, including the right to vote, to hold office, to take part in the duties of governing along with the whites, and of modifying the state governments if need for so doing should arise. These amendments rest on the doctrine, which is implied, that the previous condition of slavery prevented the exercise of rights which really existed but which under that system could have no exercise; and, what they did was to apply to the slaves those principles and protect them in the exercise of those rights on which the American polity is founded.

But, what we are chiefly concerned in is to know, as clearly as possible, what was the character of the Southern population, all of whom then were equally clothed with the rights and the corresponding duties of the citizen and all of whom irrespective of race, color, or previous servitude must henceforth exercise those rights and duties in concert.

The mixed population of the South divided and divides it still in nearly all its institutions from the more homogeneous people of the North or West. It was and is therefore a section. In round numbers there are some fourteen million whites and seven and a half million Negroes. These contrasted peoples are further apart in appearance and in physical characteristics than any two races in the world. They are not as closely related as the Germans are with the Greeks, as distant as that ancient relationship may be. They are further apart than the Anglo-Saxon is from the Indian. They have not mingled on anything like a basis of equality in the social relations, nor has any marked race fusion taken place. For 240 years these races have moreorless lived together, have had many of their interests interlaced, have occupied the same land, and mutually assisted each other. And, despite this long continued contact, so little affinity has resulted that few marriages have occurred; and, the only evidence of such a tendency is found in a class of mulattoes, octaroons, and so on, the greater part of whom are not offspring of white parents on either side, but of colored persons on both sides.[1] Thus, in the relations of the family, which are the foundations of the relations of society, in the relations of private life which lie at the basis of the relations of public life, unanimity of feeling does not exist. No relaxation of this cordon of race has taken place during recent years.

However philanthropic or optimistic in his views of human nature one may be, it is undeniable that the mere difference of race in itself creates a lack of sympathy between the peoples so differing. The white man, be he rich or poor, does not deem the black man worthy of the same regard which he considers as the white man's due. The Negro, on his part, however friendly disposed, cannot escape the feeling that the white race, as a race, is somewhat hostile; and, the interest of that race cannot be with him a matter of very deep moment. These contrasted feelings of race with race do not often display themselves with anything like violence, but they exist. All the individuals of both races know

[1] In view of what Seabrook has written previously, this appears to be contradictory. Even if here he means "legally" colored, the process of mixture must involve a considerable number of *white* parents.

their reality, and they come to the surface when fitting occasion presents itself, and they subside when the temporary occasion is past.

Originating thus largely in difference of race, the white man's lack of regard for the black and the Negro's lack of interest in the white man's behalf inevitably brings about an amount of friction in any matter where leadership or power is concerned. The Negro is apt to distrust the white, and the white to assume as matter of course the Negro's inferiority and dispute his claims to equality. In the mind of the whites the inferiority of the Negro race extends itself to all the relations of life, not only public but private as well.

But moreover, this mixed Southern population is very markedly still the product of the peculiar past which precedes it. Theoretically, of course, we all know what that past has been, but we do not realize what an immense moulding power that past has had in fixing the present conditions, feelings, habits, and relations of the two races at the South. People, however goaded by change of conditions, or spurred by ambition, or led by superior leaders, can no more escape the influences of centuries than an individual can become someone else or spring over his own shadow.

The history of the white race has been one of conquest and robbery abroad and independence at home. While subjecting other peoples to their rule by force, they have preserved for themselves the principles of free government. The different regions of the globe, however varying in soil and clime, they have invaded for their own uses and subjected to the perpetuation of their own power. The same spirit of conquest which overran England in the fifth century has remained to the present day the characteristic of the English race and at the present moment is being exhibited by them in the occupation of inhospitable Africa itself, with the possible and remote object of civilizing that continent and the immediate object of enriching themselves. True to their ancient principle, the English and kindred races have followed out in America the same policy. Hither into the colonies of the Atlantic Coast they have transported, to do their bidding, the peaceful and submissive tribes of Africa and kept them in a condition of servitude for more than two centuries.

During that period of time the races in this country have segregated themselves in obedience to the difference of climate and the difference of industries. The South became the residence of the Negroes, and the North remained the home and asylum of the white races of the Old World. At the South, where the black race has mainly collected, the whites have all along claimed as a natural right and as a right fixed by law the power of ruling the other race in almost every action of daily life. By the laws of the land the whites of every rising generation were born masters of the other race. They were reared in the habit of exercising the powers and the duties of the ruler as an inherited and inalienable right. The immense and subtle influence which this inherited and unquestioned power has upon the minds and feelings of the master race cannot be overestimated. They were rulers from their birth. They met no opposition to their sway. They, over whom their power extended, were by their nature and by force of long usage submissive, quiet, and peaceable.

These rulers knew not what was meant by compromise. They had no need of considering the rights or the advantage of the ruled beyond the limit that was fixed by their own advantage. Each man who owned slaves became the maker of law and the executor of law in his own person. In this way a class of petty sovereigns was produced whose power was absolute so far as the subject race was concerned. No sort of contest or competition existed between the slave race and the master race. The gulpf [sic] which sundered them was too vast. Between them there existed the difference of race, the difference of status, the difference of education and morals, the difference of property, and—stronger than all—a profound difference in the way of looking at life. The one race accepted the unquestioned fact that it was born to rule. The other race accepted the equally unquestioned fact that somehow it was born to serve, and it looked toward its masters with eager eyes and with dumb lips for the tokens of kindness and good will.

Here, let us pause a while and sacrifice in the temple of Justice. It is true that the power of the master race was absolute, but it is also true that the very absoluteness of that power called forth in the mind of the ruling class a feeling of kindly sympathy. No reference to the system of Negro slavery at the South can be truthful without the recognition of this vital fact. Between the owner and the slave there sprung up a bond of personal attachment far more intimate and stronger than exists between employer and employed probably anywhere else in the world. The unreasoning and childlike submission of the slave and the entire power of the master naturally created this natural bond of feeling. So real and deep-seated was this attachment that during the period of the Civil War and during the tumultuous era which has since elapsed, the allegiance of the former slave and former master still retained much of its vitality and is at the present moment a powerful factor in the preservation of peace and order.

Such are the conditions and facts which moulded the feelings and conduct of the white race toward the black prior to the period of emancipation. We will now go on to shew that since that period, violent as the change from slavery to freedom may appear, very much the same relations between race and race have existed and still exist. A small minority of the Negroes, chiefly mulattoes, many of whom were never slaves, have become practically independent of the control of the white race; but, the vast majority of them are still ruled by the whites. The character of work, the amount of work, their actions toward each other and toward the whites, educational instruction—be it in agricultural or mechanical work or in knowledge of books—their political actions are all controlled by the white race and in some cases, especially in matters political, with the same absolutism which existed in the slave era.

These then are some of the respects in which the conduct of the whites toward the blacks has been influenced by their past histories. The Negroes also are open to the operation of the same law. Their relation and behavior toward the whites are determined more by their antecedent history than by recent events of the last thirty years. The recreating of a people, however hopeful be the dream of the enthusiast, is essentially a slow work of the future and a future of changed conditions.

During the entire period in which the Negroes have enjoyed the rights of the citizen they have practically remained under the tutelage of the white race. This seems to have been a necessity of the case from which neither race could escape, even had they aimed so to do. The whites, with few exceptions, have been the directors of all the occupations of private life; and, the whites also, whether of the Republican or Democratic party, have been the rulers of the black citizens in all matters of public life. The great influence of past conditions on each race may be summed up as follows. The whites have all along been accustomed to rule the Negroes as inferiors; the Negroes have all along been used to be ruled and to accept the position of inferiors. The past life and training of each race shew these effects in the relations of the present moment, nor have these effects been legislated out of existence. If the Fifteenth Amendment of the Constitution, when it declared the "rights" of the citizen could have obliterated the effects of past conditions upon the races, the political unity of those races at the South would have been speedily reached, but such is the principle of natural progress that the change of a slave race into a race of free citizens is a slow and painful process.

The peoples of the South are further contrasted with each other by great differences of education. Some 20 percent of the whites are illiterate, and along with these are 80 to 90 percent Negro illiterates.[2] To these people the use of the public prints is practically denied, and along with this ignorance there naturally goes a large amount of suspicion. This unlettered multitude, by reason of their ignorance surrounded by doubt and uncertainty, have in their hands the power of the ballot without educational qualification. They are readily the prey of any who would advance themselves at the cost of peace and prosperity to whites and blacks indifferently. The work of getting the Negro at the South educated has only begun. The field to be covered is vast; it is also wild. It is to be noted that the blacks are to be trained into the habits of thinking of the white race. This is the goal to be reached.

Very tardily do the means of education reach that people. They are scattered over a vast extent of only partially settled country. Means of communication are often absent. The great mass of them

[2]Census figures (1890) show that in the South Atlantic region 14.5 per cent of the whites and 60.1 per cent of the Negroes over ten years of age were illiterate. This included the District of Columbia and the states of Delaware, Maryland, Virginia, West Virginia, North Carolina, South Carolina, Georgia, and Florida. Approximately the same figures—15.3 per cent and 61.2 per cent —were reported for the South Central states of Kentucky, Tennessee, Alabama, Mississippi, Louisiana, Texas, Oklahoma, and Arkansas.

live about great tracts of land and at considerable distances apart. Generally they are not united in villages but have pitched their homes, often of a very temporary nature, here and there about outlying fields on the edges of swamps or wooded tracts and many of them on almost inaccessible islands of the Southern coast. The field of work is not inviting to the school teacher, and then the pay is poor and not apt to attract the talent of competent instructors. The young generation of blacks are mostly engaged in the simplest kind of field work, the nature of which does not encourage the need or desire of knowledge and which, although poorly paid, consumes the time which might otherwise be given to school attendance. Into these remote and partially settled corners of the country the means of information do not easily find their way, and the people remain ignorant of the simple rudiments of knowledge, as well as of the business interests of their neighborhood and also of any public measures which may be attracting the attention of more intelligent classes of the state or country at large.

Nearly all the work which they do in the country and a large part of that which they do in the towns is so simple and unskilled a sort that it furnishes no spur for the acquisition of knowledge. It demands little thought and little exercise of personal responsibility. The planning of any kind of work which demands the exertion of the mental faculties is generally done by the whites and always where they are interested in the outcome. Such are the educational surroundings in which the great mass of the Southern Negroes live and die.

In addition to the above causes which retard their educational advance, the Negroes themselves add another. It is a habit with them, both in town and country, to withdraw themselves as far as possible from the presence of the other race. They are compelled to seek the company of and to intermingle with the whites for the getting of work and wages; but, that done, they manifest a desire to retire within themselves. The whites are aware of the fact that they are not welcome among them except as employers and paymasters, and soon find that otherwise they are objects of total indifference. In this way the personal friction of the white race upon the black, with whatever good influences may thus be exerted, is much retarded. The truth constantly makes itself evident that the white man's methods and ideas are not those of the other race, and the bare presence of the whites becomes and seems to be felt by them to be a criticism of their methods of life. In their present stage of advance a very large and important part of what we, from our standpoint, call civilization does not seem to be adapted to these descendants of the African tribes.

Only in a very partial way have they assimilated themselves to the life of the white race which surrounds them. Many traits of the whites they do not appreciate at all, probably because such traits are the products of a different civilization and a different race history. The religion of the whites they have absorbed in their own way and very naturally modified to suit their racial inherited feelings in these matters, and they practice their religious exercises entirely in their own way. In truth, so entirely are they segregated from whites in these matters that very few white persons really know what their religious tenets are and, if asked, could give no definite answer.

They have a rather weak sympathy with the (white man's) laws as the rules by which their conduct towards each or the whites is to be governed. Very many of these laws find no response in their moral nature. The vices of the slave—lying, stealing, conceal-ment, unchastity, and so on—are still active within them and destroy in their consciousness that moral basis on which rest the laws which are aimed against such evils. In their eyes, the white man is un-reasonable and cruel who forces upon them a close observance of any laws which are based upon his peculiar habits and feelings.

An example will illustrate the truth referred to. If an article of personal property is set aside and remains unused, it is very likely that it will be appropriated by some Negro or other. The owner claims that it is "stolen" and calls the act of taking it a "theft." The Negro says, on his part and in unison with his ideas or lack of ideas, that it was not stolen, it was only "taken." And, from his standpoint, the act is pardonable, natural, a verdict which very often the owner finds it best and wisest to accept. And the same kind of reasoning (or feeling) characterizes the Negro in the doing of many other things. In this condition of moral inertia it often and usually happens that when the laws are put into force as against the blacks, they readily take for granted that the punishment is unjust, and the feeling excited in their minds is not one of humiliation, but of indifference or contempt. Thus the enforcement of the laws fails of full remedial effect and illustrates very completely the inherent difficulty of forcing not one people, but two unequally developed races to live (perhaps to exist at all) under the same institutions.

There is, in truth, a constant moral compromise going on between race and race. The ill will of the Negro is being often unavoidably stirred up, and the impatience of the whites has frequent cause for its exhibition. But, if the Negroes at the South are not distinguished by the exercise of private morals to any serious extent, as all the world knows, on what rational ground shall we demand that they shall exercise those public morals which are incumbent upon the citizen in the performance of his public duties by which not only himself but often others are to be affected? Justice, the habit of guarding the rights of others, is probably the highest quality of man and the citizen; and this, as well as the other elements that make up reliable public character, like charity, begin at home. They have their roots in influences of daily life. They cannot be put on for use on public occasions only.

We now approach a phase of character of the Southern population which still further distinguishes it. While it is true that the white people of the South distrust the Negroes' exercise of political rights, the further truth must be added that the Negroes on their part do not shew any real appreciation of those rights. They do not understand their value and, not having won or made them for themselves, are not keenly interested in preserving them. In fact, it seems very likely that if the agitation of the Negro vote were discontinued by the Republican party, the Negroes of themselves would drop their interest in matters political. The whole mental disposition of the race, due to causes as before set forth, tends to keep them in the condition of subjection. Intelligent and rigorous assertion by them of their rights is not their habit. Too readily do they accept whatever place chance and the power of the whites choose to assign to them. Lack of ambition on their part is marked; and, if they are conscious of the reality of their public rights and duties, the expression of such consciousness is not marked enough to impress the observer with a belief in its reality.

The Negroes of the South have been so long used to the rule of others that they do not admire or believe in the whites who come down to their level, or pretend to do so. Like other partly savage races, the shew of force has for them charms which are incomprehensible to the freeman. Respect for the white man is curiously in proportion to the power which the white man is able to exert. Their conduct will not allow one to believe that they are to any extent amenable to the *rule of reason;* but, they will lead him to see, though he be loath so to do, that the rule of force and the ability to carry it out is the method which they best understand.

The Negroes are supple, docile, and inert so far as the whites are concerned, but sometimes quarrelsome and intractible among themselves. They habitually imitate the whites, and this the whites know and count on. However valuable their services may be, it does not seem to occur to the whites to consult the Negro's wishes, to ask his opinion, or seek his cooperation except on very rare occasions. Whenever the question of equality comes up, the segregation of the races, to use a very mild expression, is quite complete. An inferior and superior civilization are here going on side by side and interlaced with each other—a state of things which is un-American and glaringly contrasted with the political and social polity of the country at large.

It is a matter of daily observation that the great mass of the Southern Negroes are deplorably poor, almost too poor to call their liberty their own from day to day. But unfortunately, all over the world, even where popular government is supposed to exist, liberty of the individual is largely expressed in terms of dollars and cents. We know that in the England of early days, in that fierce and predatory society, so keen was often the struggle of life that want repeatedly forced the freeman to throw aside his liberty and become a voluntary slave. He gave up the sword and the spear and humbly took up the mattock, thenceforth to be wielded in the interest of a master.

The poverty of the blacks in the South has, in a general way, forced them to do the same thing. A condition of *serfdom* has to a great extent followed the condition of *slavery*. In many localities the Negro freedmen are as completely attached to the land on which and by which they live and as subject to the owner of the soil as the class of serfs everywhere; and, the striking part of the relation is this, that if the proprietor is fairly interested in their welfare and governed by kindly sentiments towards them, this somewhat feudal relation seems to be quite satisfactory, and no jar or cause of complaint arises. This poverty of the Negroes at the South, as well as that of a large proportion of the white population, is not due to political causes of any sort, nor yet to the results of a civil war. It has its true source in the primitive condition of labor and the primitive condition of industries. The old incubus of ignorant and underpaid work, the old system of unambitious and unimproving work has left its fatal marks upon the entire people both black and white; and, moreover, the stock of Southerners, especially descendants of the slavery regime, are intensely conservative, skeptical of any good results which may come of new employment, and apt to call any change an experiment.

The lack of a diversified labor is a great cause of the poor financial condition of both races, particularly the Negroes. The financial condition of the workers, the wages which they are able to get and save, depends on the division of work; and, the possibility of such division depending upon the skill and intelligence of the workers, it follows that upon the acquirement of this intelligence hangs the well-being of the employed. And yet, one is impressed on all hands with the fact that the great simplicity of the chief occupation of the South precludes the need of a diverse intelligence and really affords in this way a barrier to improvement in the condition of the toilers. One more remark in this connection and we will pass on to a different phase of the matter.

There is a complicated and abnormal contest going on all over this section. There is some slight trace of the usual struggle of the employed and employer; the natural conflict of work and wages. But, this conflict is involved by the fact that the employed are divided against themselves. This abnormal state of things has its rise in difference of race. The white workman finds that he must compete with the black workman and in many kinds of industry finds himself underbid. His rate of wages is apt to be reduced and his chances of employment lessened. This competition brings about by far the keenest sense of conflict of race with race and [is] *based on the characteristics of race* which shews itself at the

South. It affects the actions of the white man, be he Southern or Northern, native or emigrant, toward the black man directly and profoundly. It destroys his feelings of good will, and it lessens his sense of justice. He thinks it a hardship that he should be forced into competition with an inferior race, and it stirs his anger. It draws the race line harder and sharper, and the black man comes to be looked upon as an intruder who were much better out of the way. In addition, then, to the other differences which exist between the two peoples, we must add the further difference in the character of work and amount of pay, resulting in a conflict which is directly based on difference of race and is intensified thereby.

"The South" is a very misleading expression. In the minds of most people it usually means the white race there. This assumption is very natural and very far from the truth. It is, in fact, a violently contrasted conglomeration of two races who do not assimilate and who do not live on the same plane of life, either physical or mental. In the modern sense of the word, these races form only a partly civilized society. For a real civilization looks and ought to look to the betterment not of a class nor of a minority of the people, but of the entire population. Not the aggrandizement, but the diffusion of knowledge, of good morals, of privilege, and of means is the true goal of any civilization which would be in accord with the Nineteenth century. The very rich man by [the] side of the beggar, the learned by the side of the illiterate, the absolute ruler by the side of the grinning slave is essentially a medieval state of life. Civilization means that the rule of force has yielded to the rule of reason, and it means that the ruled have the ability to claim and exercise a share in the business of governing the actions of the society of which they form a part. It is a matter of easy observation that the people of the South, including both races, have a great deal to learn in all those things moral, intellectual, and material which make up civilization. Of civilization, popular freedom is one of the last and most perishable fruits. It has not sprung in very full perfection from the soil of which we are speaking. It has tended to become the privilege of a class rather than the property of the people. Such then is the South and such are the conditions under which state governments by the people are supposed to be maintained.

Now, although these two races are marked by so many contrasts, there is by law equality of civil and political rights. The rights of the black citizens are set forth and protected by legislation. But, is that all? Could legislation do no more? Is its action rather negative and confined to setting forth that "the right of citizens shall not be denied etc."? So it seems. The limits in which legislation can exert itself are fixed by natural causes. The act of declaring the rights of the citizen does not create the qualities of the citizen. Declaration of rights is within the power of legislation, while the conferring or creating of the qualities which make the citizen is not within the power of any legislation whatsoever. A glance at the various enactments on this subject will illustrate this truth.

Article xv [of the] U.S. Constitution. "The right of U.S. citizen to vote shall not be denied on account of race, color, or previous condition of servitude." Here the right of the citizen is declared, but the law makes no attempt (nor pretence of any) to remove either the (mental) characteristic of race nor those effects which that previous condition of servitude has produced. Again, "All men are born free and equal with inalienable rights, among which are the rights of . . . acquiring and protecting property, etc." Here again is the declaration of rights, but the industry and ability needed to acquire that property, being natural powers of the individual, are not conferrable by law.

"All political power is vested in and derived from the people." Therefore they have the right to modify their form of government as they may deem expedient, etc. Here again is the same thing. The ability to know what is public good and the skill in affairs requisite to modify government accordingly are based upon the sense and virtue of the people and may or may not exist.

"No person shall be prevented from acquiring education, etc." True, but the mental power to acquire education and the desire to do so inhere in the individual, and whether he exert them or not rests finally with the man. The object of the Reconstruction legislation has been to remove the obstacles to the improvement of the Negro citizens of the South. It has not proceeded upon the idea that the law could confer upon them by some shorthand process that improvement itself. It has declared their rights as citizens, but has not conferred upon them the habits, the intelligence or the means upon which an effective citizenship rests. All these things have not been done by law because law-making could not do them. What remains to be done, and it is by far the greater part of the work of raising the Negro race to the plane of higher life, does not come within the province of laws of any sort. The chance for progress has been furnished the Negro, not by attempting to measure it out to them by the pound, but by removing the old burden of *slavery as a legal status* under which the race lived in unambition and stagnation. The Negroes' field for exertion has been cleared, their road to betterment has been opened. The duty of walking therein and reaching their journey's end thenceforth depends on themselves.

It is time to change the character of the talk on this whole subject, time to stop imagining all sorts of intentions on the part of the statesmen of the North, setting forth that they have attempted to do impossibilities and then criticizing such supposed intentions on the ground that they have failed. It is rather a childish argument to build a man of straw with the transparent intention of again knocking it down. It is absurd to assume that the public men of the North aimed by the Reconstruction laws to suddenly create a new society, or to rule the Southern states by means of their poverty and ignorance, or that they believed seriously that the differences of intelligence, morals, means, and the inherited prejudices of centuries would be obliterated by the passing of amendments to the Constitution. Or, that they believed that the multitudes only yesterday freed from a lazy sort of slavery which has been the life of the Negro tribes for several thousand years were competent to grasp and control the governments of states. Presumptions of this sort and talk of this sort springs from the rhetorical temper of the Southern man, no doubt due somewhat to the heat of the climate and the rigor of the sun.

But, it is somewhat surprising to find the author of *An Appeal to Caesar*, Judge Tourgée, who is a Republican, speaking as follows: "The failure of the Reconstruction Acts to accomplish the results which their authors anticipated must be admitted by everyone. . . . The responsibility for this failure rests entirely with the people and statesmen of the North. . . . The duty which devolved upon the people and legislators of the North at the close of the war was the obliteration of those differences which had so long separated the two peoples. . . . The task which devolved upon the victor was to unify the nation in spirit as well as in form." [3] The first remark to be made is that these views do not agree with the remarks of the same author in the latter part of his very strong and interesting book.

As to the Reconstruction Acts, it is not so clear that they so completely failed, unless we assume as Judge Tourgée seems to do, that they were aimed at impossible results. In the next place, the responsibility for the supposed failure does not rest with the people and statesmen of the North for this good and strong reason, that the condition of the Negroes here was the result of causes which legislation by its very nature could not reach. One cause, for instance, is the mental inertia of the Negroes themselves; another is the lazy habit of subjection which seems to have always been a product of Africa. In short, the Reconstruction measures had poor material on which to work. The task, whose now fulfillment he deplores, "of unitizing the nation in spirit as well as form" meets the same kind of difficulty.

What now is the answer to the question with which these pages set out? Are the conditions at the South favorable for the maintaining of governments "by the people"—bearing in mind that it is the *people* who are concerned. This question has been partly answering itself all along. The fact is, and one quite apparent to all, that the governments of the Southern states, particularly those where the Negro race is collected in great force, are not governments by the people in any complete sense of the term. The cause is apparent. In these states a large part of the voting population—and in three of them a majority of that population—although possessing the rights of citizens do not yet possess and have not acquired in the short period of their liberty what may be called the qualities of citizens. The Negroes shew a lack of

[3]See Albion W. Tourgée, *An Appeal to Caesar* (New York, 1884), 68–69. Tourgée, an Ohio-born author and judge, is best known for his career as a carpetbagger in North Carolina and his books about his experiences, especially *Fool's Errand* (1879). See Otto H. Olsen, *Carpetbagger's Crusade: The Life of Albion W. Tourgée* (Baltimore, 1956).

interest and a lack of ability, and the whites, to whatever class they belong, have no faith in the exercise of power by the other race. The state and local governments based upon the conditions which we have aimed to set forth become governments not only of a race, but of a class of that race and are controlled by minorities. The principle of majority rule has not worked it out with any success as applied to this heterogeneous population.

A difficulty is hidden, or is believed to be hidden, in the very heart of the matter. When a society accepts the method of majority rule and as a result the minority submits itself to the power of the majority, there exists the tacit belief among them that their interests are so identical, their common aims so similar in the main, that the control of the lesser number by the greater will not bring about injury or loss to those so controlled. On the other hand, when the society is composed of unequal and discordant elements whose interests are not or are believed not to be identical, a minority—if they have the power so to do—will resist or defeat the rule of majorities and abandon that political principle in order to avoid what may be greater evils.

The criticism most likely to be made upon the views herein set forth is that they are negative in their character. Space has been given to shewing what the peoples of the South have not done and cannot do, rather than what they have done or may be able to do. And, as to the black race of the South, the position has been held that while they possess the rights of citizens, they do not exhibit the qualities of citizens. It has been shewn that the Reconstruction Acts have, by the very nature of the case, done but half the work of raising the Negro population to the plane of white life which is the end to be reached. In short, that the two peoples are still two peoples who have not become equalized in the relations of private life, nor yet in the relations of public life.

Will it be said then, in view of these facts, that the amendments of the U.S. Constitution have been a mere idle experiment of legislators born of fanaticism and ignorance of the conditions with which they were dealing? By no means, for the opposite of the conclusions will be seen to contain much of truth. For, if the Reconstruction measures did not create a body of full-fledged citizens, they removed past disabilities and gave them helps and incentives to become so. If they did not wipe out the effects of a dark past of servitude, they shed some light on the road to a brighter future. If they did not succeed in injecting intelligence into the Negro masses, they made public schools and at least offered the means of knowledge to those who had the faculty to receive it. If they did not remove the poverty of the Negroes, they raised them from their life of unpaid toil and made it possible for them to demand wages and truely acquire the means of self-support, self-respect, and independence.

These are some of the things which the Reconstruction measures did with success. As we look back at the history of the Negroes and at their present condition, it seems to grow clear that the last two benefits named—the means of education and the chance of earning money—are of vastly greater intrinsic value to that race than the right of suffrage. The right of the ballot in the hands of the ignorant and the poor is everywhere largely controlled by the few who possess skill and power and wealth, but the benefits of knowledge and the blessings of financial independence are rather more the property of the individual and lie at the base of every kind of advance in the life of the people. As education and means increase among the Negroes, a better use and a fuller appreciation of their public rights will naturally follow, but that it should precede these things is demanding more of the possibilities of human nature than human nature can achieve.

The "right to acquire property" does not end with itself, but brings about other results of a moral sort. What has this right done for the black citizens? It has enabled them to make homes for themselves for the first time in their history. It has allowed them to spend the earnings of their work upon the improvement of their home life. The making of a home, however rude, is a civilizing influence of great power. It carries along with it the sense of independence. It begets self-respect which is the foundation of better habits. It creates a desire for better things. It teaches the first duties of the citizen, respect for other's rights and some regard for the laws by which the safety of society is preserved. It helps to beget a feeling of personal pride, a desire for further enlightenment, and a standing of social respectability. These are the tendencies and results which come of the right to acquire property, tendencies farther reaching in their ability to make a class of good citizens than the highly artificial right to cast the ballot.

And, there are other benefits which are also brought about. The community at large, as well as that of the Negroes, is directly concerned. Among the Negroes there has gradually grown up a class of professional men, doctors, lawyers, and preachers of the Gospel, all of whom have an incentive to seek the means of improvement and prosecute their callings. These signs of advance among the freedmen are shewing themselves all over the South, and they prove very clearly that the period of freedom has not been without its fruits of progress. With facts of this kind before us, it cannot be said that the Reconstruction efforts deserve to be classed among the legislative blunders of the country.[4]

---

[4]Seabrook originally terminated his discussion at this point, signing his name "I. D. Seabrook, Mills House, Charleston, S.C."

6

Looking Forward

Everywhere throughout these pages the same truth has been making itself apparent. Whether we studied the Negro population of the South as moulded by the influence of slavery or as affected by the better conditions which have existed since, whether we have examined the character of their occupations and the amount of knowledge which they may have gotten in this way, whether we have regarded their natural ability for the receiving of education, or whether we have looked at the amount of their property or their ability to exercise the duties of the citizen and the kind of training which they have had therein, the same truth has presented itself. That truth is this: that while the colored race possess the rights of the citizen, they do not possess equally with the other [race] what we have called the qualities of the citizen; and that hence, the fundamental condition for the exercise of such rights in their case is largely absent. If this is the disease, its removal consists in the Negroes' acquiring these qualities of the citizen. This is the only solution which will be radical enough to merit the name of a solution at all.

We have attempted to analyze the condition of the Negroes at the South and have found that a political equality of any reality does not coexist along with moral inequality, educational inequality, and a general inequality in the traits which make the citizen. What,

then, is the problem of the future? It is nothing less than the raising of the Negro population to the plane of white life. Not a part,
but the total life of that people must be elevated. We have seen that
the acquisition of the rights of the citizen, without the intelligence
of the citizen, is only a half possession; and, we have seen too
that moral power is interwoven with political power and is largely
the basis on which it rests. So deeply connected are all the relations of human life that the improvement of one presupposes the
improvement of the others, and the defect of one speedily brings
about the defect of the rest.

When the philanthropist says, "The slaves are free; they are
henceforth free men;" or, when the statesman says, "The freemen
are now citizens; they will henceforth exercise their rights;" we
have seen that both philanthropist and statesman may be mis-
taken. For the freeman may not value or preserve his liberty, and
the citizen may lack the moral force to exercise his rights. How
then are the Negro citizens to acquire the qualities of the citizen
which as yet they so imperfectly possess? Or, to put the question
in its more general form, how is the black population of the
South to reach the plane of white life which surrounds them, so
that they shall become not perpetual inferiors but a homogeneous
part of that life. By a betterment of the conditions under which
they are living and a moral growth of the people themselves.

We have seen what the Reconstruction measures achieved in
the work of raising the level of Negro life, how they removed
some of the difficulties in the way of progress and opened the
road to advance, leaving necessarily to the Negroes themselves
the task of following that road, the ultimate result being essentially a thing of the future.

Under the better circumstances of the last twenty years the
black race at the South has been gradually moving forward. They
have increased their amount of worldly goods. They have gained
in knowledge and to some extent diversified their employments.
Influenced by a continuance of the conditions and forced forward
by the growth of the industrial life of the section, it is natural
to suppose that their improvement will go on. And here two
important questions present themselves. It will be asked, "How
will a material advance among them produce a moral advance, the

very thing most needed." And, secondly, "How will a material advance help to allay that feeling of race prejudice which exists against them so strongly in the breasts of the whites?"

As to the first question, in a preceding chapter while discussing the results of the Reconstruction measures, we had occasion to dwell upon the obvious fact, the greatest benefit which those laws conferred upon the freedman was the "right to acquire property," because such acquirement of property shews a direct tendency to increase among them a sense of self-respect, and to raise the tone of morals, to foster a regard for the law, and to beget an interest in the welfare of the society among which they live, and that this moral improvement produces among the whites a proper respect for those blacks who possess it. Thus, the material advance of the Negro citizens, by helping forward a moral advance, tends steadily to bring about a unanimity of the races by diminishing the contrasts which have hitherto divided them.

As to the second question, will the material advance of the Negroes allay the feeling of race prejudice which exists among the whites? In many Southern communities there is a growing minority of thrifty and well-to-do Negroes. These people respect themselves and naturally call forth respect of others. They regard the rights of others and look to have their own rights correspondingly regarded. They know and observe the distinctions of race and do so without manifesting an ever-present sense of offensive hostility. Their intercourse with the whites is neither sullen, nor rude, nor unreasoning. They are reliable and honest. They are wise enough to know that the white man's civilization and methods are matters of immense value to them. And, they possess sufficient insight to perceive that the right to vote does not bind them to either party, which, in the present and past state of Negro politics, is a proof of a very great intelligence indeed. In short, this class among the Negroes has reached a higher plane of civilization and forms a real part of the life of their respective communities.

Now, the fact is that toward this class of blacks the race prejudice of the whites seldom shews itself because there are no causes calculated to call it into existence. The harmony is as complete as under the circumstances is possible and that attitude of mind which is called "race conflict" may be said hardly to exist. These things are matters of fact, open to the observation of the candid enquirer; and, they point to the truth that as the Negro citizens approach the plane of white life and absorb white civilization they are "treated white" as they express it. The asperities and dislikes between the races tend to lessen and mollify themselves. This, then, is the answer to the question. The fact that those individuals of the Negro race who in reaching a higher level of life have thereby climbed above the influence of race prejudice leads us to conclude that it is possible at some future day, by a process of natural selection, for the better elements of the Negro population—having risen from their present state of life on its low level—to climb also above the atmosphere of racial antipathy and render possible a greater unity of the Southern people. That the blacks shall attain the qualities of citizens, that the plane of Negro life shall be raised to the plane of white life presupposes several conditions:

I. The first is that the Negroes shall remain in contact with the white race. The influence or stimulus of the white race upon them must go on. For, if the Negro is expelled by the whites or if in any way the whites are ousted by the Negroes, in either case contact of the races will cease and at [the] same time will also cease the impulse to improvement which the superior race has all along been exercising upon the inferior. The truth of this position is apparent. For, even in the period of servitude, a sort of training of the servile race was in progress and to its results is largely due the ability of the Negroes to maintain themselves since. At the present moment all that the black citizens have, whether it be better habits, methods of work, or property, or the laws by which they are protected from each other, everything in fine which they have gained of civilization has been forced upon them by the influence of the other race, and to a great extent without their consent or assistance.

One may confidently assert that there is, as yet, nothing distinctively Negro in this country, unless it be a dim remnant of the African creeds, the influence of which still seems to exist. On their own behalf and as free of white influence that people has originated or accomplished little in this land. If we are to guess the future from the facts of the past, it is likely that the Africans in America, if divorced from the stimulating and controlling presence of the whites, will re-enact their usual record of inefficiency or even retrogression. Their performances under rather favorable circumstances in Hayti [*sic*], Jamaica, and in some sections of the Southern coast where they are collected in great numbers are too well-known to require comment. The philanthropist is not encouraged by the results wrought out in these settlements.

Frequently in the preceding pages our attention has been called to the fact that the blacks in the South are still much under the control of the white population, even in localities where the whites are in a very small minority. We have seen the reason for this state of things. We found the cause to consist in the fact that in all the employments of the town and country whites are compelled to take upon themselves the troublesome duty of director and instructor, not because they have any special hankering for doing all this, but because in no other way can success in these industries be assured. There is another reason why the elevation of the Negroes is conditioned by their continuance among the whites. It is to be remembered that the plane of life which they must reach is that of the white race. A Negro civilization is not the goal to be attained. Now it is inconceivable to the mind of any intelligent observer that this somewhat distance goal would ever be arrived at by them if their race were collected in mass within the limits of any territory or state. Should this segregation of race occur, the leaven of the white man would cease to act among them; for the whites would not invade such territory; or rather, only those would go thither whose influence would be of the worst kind. While, on the other hand, the better class of Negroes would refuse to go thither altogether because they would prefer to remain in the region of civilization.

II. The second condition requisite for the elevation of that race is that the limit of race improvement among them shall be the same as that of the whites; or, that at least there shall be no natural bar preventing their improvement from going on indefinitely. No one now living, whatever his personal knowledge of the Negroes, can honestly say that he knows whether there be such a limit or not. The period of their repression has been so long and the era of their free activity has been so short that in this country at least there are no data [on which] to base a conclusion.

Of course, as matter of argument, it may be contended that if that people had within them any power of extended progress they never would have been as they always have the great slave race of the world; while, on the other hand, and with great force it may be held that the region of central Africa, by reason of its climate, is so hostile to the growth of a strong race that there only the lowest form of life is possible, that of slavery and barbarism; and, it may be true that the European race itself, if subjected for a long period to the same conditions, would degenerate into the same state. But, whatever be the scientific truth about the problem of race limits, it is to be hoped, both for the sake of the white race, the benefit of the country, and for the sake of the Negroes themselves, that they will in this country take occasion by the hand and cease to shew their ancient lack of progressive power. This matter of possible race limitations is mentioned here, not with any hope of throwing new light upon its mysteries, shrouded as it is in the dark shadows of a long past, but only to emphasize the fact that if such limits in the case of the Negro do exist the settlement of the Negro problem in the U.S. must remain an impossibility, because the equalization of the two peoples can never be realized.

III. The third condition essential to the elevation of the Negro race is akin to the first. It is that the numerical increase of that race shall not so far exceed that of the whites as to practically convert part of the South into Negro states. There does not appear to be any reason to think that this event will ever happen. The Eleventh Census, that of 1890, sets out the following facts with regard to the relative percentage of the Negro to the white population of the South, including the South Central and South Atlantic divisions during the century elapsing between 1790 and 1890.

In 1790 the relative percentage of the Negro to the white population in the South, including the states from Delaware to Arkansas, was 25.64.[1] In 1860, the end of the period during which the rear-

[1] Seabrook includes here, of course, parts of the continent which were not within the boundaries of the United States in 1790. Figures in these pages are cited from *The Compendium of the Eleventh Census: 1890* (Washington, 1892), I, xcviii–cv.

ing of slaves was a monied interest and care was taken by slave owners to increase the number as much as possible, this relative percentage had risen to 36.85. In 1890, thirty years later, comprising a period during which slavery was at an end and the rearing of slaves was no longer a monied interest or business, the percentage of the Negro to the white population has fallen to 33.77.

There is thus shewn for the South at large during the last thirty years a decrease of the Negro population compared with the white. During this period of time, however, comprising thirty years in which the Negroes no longer in slavery were free to mass and locate themselves as clime and soil best suited their needs, they have tended to congregate in five Southern states, and in these states the percentage of the Negro to the white population has slightly increased. These states are South Carolina, where the percentage has increased from 58.59 to 59.85 of the entire population; Georgia, from 44.05 to 46.74; Mississippi, from 55.28 to 57.58; Louisiana, from 49.49 to 49.99; and Arkansas, from 25.55 to 27.40.[2]

Thus the last census shews in these five states alone a small relative increase for a period of thirty years ranging from one half to two percent. But further, a decrease even here has lately begun to shew itself, for in three of these five states, and those very highly adapted to be the habitat of the Negro, there has been an actual decline in the last ten years in this percentage of increase as follows: in South Carolina, there has been a decline of about 5000 Negroes to every 100,000 of the white population; in Alabama, a decline of 9000 Negroes to every 100,000 of the white population; and in Louisiana, a decline of 6000. In Mississippi and Arkansas the slight increase before mentioned has gone on as follows: in Mississippi during the last ten years there has been an increase of 640 Negroes to every 100,000 of the white population; and in Arkansas, an increase of 2144 Negroes to each 100,000 of the whites.

[2]In 1890 there were obviously Southern states with a greater percentage of Negroes than Arkansas. What Seabrook means is that the states he cites are those showing a definite *increase* in colored citizens, 1860–90. (And, he might have included the District of Columbia which had a thirty-year increase from 19.07 to 32.80 per cent.) During those same years, these states had a percentage decrease as indicated: Alabama, 45.40 to 44.84; Florida, 44.63 to 42.46; North Carolina, 36.42 to 34.67; Texas, 30.27 to 21.84; Tennessee, 25.50 to 24.37.

Further, the Negroes exceed the whites in numbers and have done so for a long time in only three states—South Carolina, Mississippi, and Louisiana. While in two of these states, South Carolina and Louisiana, there has been the decrease in the last decade just mentioned. When it is remembered that the states lying upon the Gulf Coast are semitropical and well adapted in soil, clime, and atmospheric humidity to the African race and in large areas much more so than to the whites, it is rather remarkable that the proportion of this population should shew so slight a variation, in some cases so small a relative gain and in others a small but actual loss.

It does not appear, then, from the census that the increase of the race in any state or states of the South is so marked as to end by creating black states whose dark masses shall become impervious to the light of civilization. On the contrary, the white and black races of the far South appear to have kept pretty well abreast of each other. Unless the industries of the locality change very suddenly, which is not probable, although the proportion of manufactures to agriculture has made some advance, it is fair to expect that the Negroes will go on locating at the far South and that their numbers will go on increasing, fairly holding their own in the future with the white population, but not doing more.

The causes which tend to localize the Negroes at the South and keep up their relative percentage of the population are easy to point out. In the first place they are adapted to its soil, its atmosphere, its products, and its labor, all of which they regard with characteristic satisfaction, without criticism and without shewing much desire to change or improve. They are not a people who are apt to become dissatisfied and emigrate because the adventurous spirit, the ambitious spirit, the keen desire of personal advance are not with them, as with other peoples, strong and disturbing passions. Nor is there any desire at the South that they should leave the section.

Furthermore, they understand the Southern white man and he understands them. This consciousness is an inheritance of the past and is not easily broken down. At the South they know where they are. The distinctions of race have been so long practised that they have become second nature and form a basis of friendly association which is recognized by both peoples. But more potent than any of these causes is the fact that the nature of most work at the

South places them in possession of the field and defeats outside competition. White emigration southward is hence warded off, not only because the Negro is already here and aims to stay, but because the emigrant cannot compete with him in his low wages and simple way of living.

Such are the causes which localize the Negroes at the South, and now as to the matter of race increase with which we are concerned. They have grown in numbers since the war from four and a half to seven and a half millions. To what shall this increase be assigned? To the comfort and affluence of their lives? Clearly not, seeing that neither comfort nor affluence is theirs. On the contrary, their means of living is meagre and often uncertain from day to day; their houses dirty and ill ventilated, and that in a hot climate; their food coarse; their medical attendance not of the best and often not called in at all, or only as a last resort. It is not the primitive character of their life, for the old idea that the partly civilized is healthier then the more advanced people has of recent years been abandoned by those who are best informed on such matters, it having been shewn as a result of greater acquaintance with various tribes that health and strength and vitality go along with better clothes, better food, and better shelter. That this is true of the Negroes in the aggregate is shewn by the well-known greater mortality among them which sometimes exceeds that of the whites by twenty-five percent. Mere race fertility, then, operating under often unfavorable conditions, is not the explanation. The cause lies elsewhere.

The true explanation is to be found in the moral habits of the race, in their view of life and its aims as seen from their standpoint. When among the whites anywhere, except in a very degraded class, an illegitimate child is born, the event is a misfortune and regarded as a proof of ungoverned lust and folly on the part of the mother. The future of the child is dark. It is possibly disowned by its family and may be a burden on society. The mother's prospects of marriage are destroyed. In case of the Negro mother and her illegitimate child, these results do not follow. To her, the fatherless child will in a few years become an acquisition, if it be a male. Her family does not disown it or her, nor is it at all apt to be left by stealth on someone's doorstep, a helpless but not silent suppliant for charity. Nor are the innocent mother's chances of marriage at all impeded by this very common and natural offspring of her youthful energies.

The question of moral wrong, of disgrace, of unchastity does not awake in the mind. How can she be unchaste in her estimate of conduct if chastity and unchastity are not distinguished in the feelings? How can disgrace arise without an ability to feel shame in both the doer and those who regard the deed? As a perfectly natural result of this primitive, almost innocent way of looking at life, legal marriage is not regarded as essential, and any of the women of proper age may be engaged in bearing children, or are willing to do so. And here again, once more are we brought back to the truth so often arrived at and from different standpoints in these pages, that the Southern question in its last analysis is based on difference of race, a difference which exhibits itself in the sexual relation as in other respects.

We must conclude, then, that despite the greater death rate among them and despite the poorer physical surroundings of their lives, their race maintains its rate of increase on account of the absence of those traits which belong to higher peoples and which in the case of the white race retard the irresponsible bearing of children and limit race growth. There is no reason to suppose that illegitimacy among them will become a crime or even a cause of moral disgrace or that improvident rearing of children, regardless of the future, will rapidly diminish. Nor is there any reason one can see, considering the natural fertility and adaption of the Southern belt, to doubt that the Negro will remain in the same large proportion there and in some parts of it peculiarly suited to his needs and way of life a majority of the people. There the climate invites them. The earth fills their simple wants and suckles them through life almost without toil; the winter breathes mildly upon them. True children of nature, they will everywhere obey the promptings of the ever-present mother with unquestioning fatalism, be the result life or death, or poverty or abundance. We may be certain that the great Southern training school of the Negro race will always be full.

In the meantime while the racial problem is working itself slowly and painfully forward, as must naturally be the case, another

important fact is becoming prominent in our national life. Whether
or not the numerical increase of the black race will retard by mere
force of numbers the increase of their civilization, which it may
or may not do, in the meantime a more complete unity of the
South, the North, and West is going on. The causes of sectional
war are gone. What Calhoun has aptly called "the warfare of legislation" is at an end with the death of that institution which called
it into life. The "warfare" in Congress against the receiving of
"anti-slavery petitions," the warfare against sectional government
patronage, the warfare against the acquiring of new territory, and
the long continued warfare of the medieval South against the
growth of the human mind itself—all these embittered contests
have fled from the political battle field. Slavery and its long control of the government are dead. The war of destiny between the
Southern nation and the Northern nation, as they were at that time,
has been fought and ended without any violent changes of the Constitution, except the abandonment of the Old Compromise between slavery and freedom, a compromise always troublesome and
impossible to preserve.

The South has no longer any "peculiar institution" to protect
and is altogether freer and lighter for having escaped the load.
The business classes of the North, the government, and laws are
no longer called upon to uphold the Southern slave holders on pain
of secession and of war. The old harassing struggles over the "bal-
ance of power," as though the country was composed of two
adjacent and hostile nations, have lost their cause for existence.
The South no longer speaks of "Northern aggression" and "Southern
submission," of "Yankee abolitionism" and "Southern vassals." New
states may now be formed without provoking violent discussions as
to whether they shall be "slave" or "free." And, it is found that
any man now of any section may remove thither with all his property and belongings. The change in Southern labor has diversified
its industries and tended to destroy the never-ending tariff contests. What was once in the days of Hamilton the "American
experiment" has become the American success. The general government has gained in strength and in recognition among the people.

White unity in this land is completer now than at any time during
this century and must increase as the result of the interwined

interests of the country. Even the old war feelings are dying out in the minds of the younger generation, as by the wide light of after events they realize the darkness of the civil struggle. No new cause of sectional conflict, which one may see, is now existent for merely economic questions will not easily bring it about.

The growth of unity between the sections in this government will have a powerful bearing upon the future of the Negro race in this country. For, if as a result of rapid race increase or other cause, the black race shall fail to coalesce with the whites and a race issue of any strength or extent arise, such an issue must assume a national, not merely local, character and must exist then, more distinctly than now, as between race and race. It is unreasonable to suppose that, no cause of sectional quarrel existing, the whites of either section would combine with the Negroes as against the whites of the other section. The Negro Question as a distinctively Southern Question will cease, and the Negro Question as a National Question will take its place. It is in part so now, but is not clearly recognized because no event has lately occurred to emphasize this new fact.

INDEX